# Super Cheap Adelaide Travel Guide 2021

"Vacations are like sleep: you need to take them regularly to benefit."

- Jessica de Bloom, a psychologist at the University of Tampere and vacation researcher.

# Our Mission

Did you know you can fly on a private jet for $500? Yes, a fully private jet. Complete with flutes of champagne and reclinable creamy leather seats. Your average billionaire spends $20,00 on the exact same flight. You can get it for $500 when you book private jet empty leg flights. Amazed? Don't be. This is just one of thousands of ways you can travel luxuriously on a budget.

When our brain hears the word "budget" it hears deprivation, suffering, agony, even depression. But budget travel need not be synonymous with hostels and pack lunches. You can enjoy an incredible and luxurious trip to Adelaide on a budget, just like you can enjoy a private jet flight for 10% of the normal cost when you know how. The past years have shown us travel is a gift we must cherish. We believe strongly that this gift is best enjoyed on a budget. Together with thrifty locals, we have funneled our passion for travel bargains into Super Cheap Adelaide.

Our passion is finding travel bargains. This doesn't mean doing less or sleeping in hostels. Someone who spends A LOT on travel hasn't planned or wants to spend their money. We promise you that with a bit of planning, you can experience a luxury trip to Adelaide on a budget.

Traveling need not be expensive; Travel guides, Travel agents, Travel bloggers and influencers often show you overpriced accommodation, restaurants and big-ticket attractions because they earn commission from your "we're on vacation" mentality, which often leads to reckless spending. Our mission is to teach you how to enjoy more for less and get the best value from every dollar you spend in Adelaide.

Taking a trip to Adelaide is not just an outer journey, it's an inner one. Budget travel brings you closer to locals, culture and authenticity; which makes your inner journey more fulfilling.

Super Cheap Adelaide will save you 1000 times what you paid for it while teaching you local tips and tricks. We have formulated a system to pass on to you, so you can enjoy a luxurious trip to Adelaide without the nightmare credit card bill.

Our mission is to dispel myths, save you tons of money, give you the local tips and tricks and help you find experiences in Adelaide that will flash before your eyes when you come to take your last breath on this beautiful earth.

# Who this book is for and why anyone can enjoy budget travel

There is a big difference between being cheap and frugal. Who doesn't like to spend money on beautiful experiences?

Over 20 years of travel has taught me I could have a 20 cent experience that will stir my soul more than a $100 one. Of course, sometimes the reverse is true, my point is, spending money on travel is the best investment you can make but it doesn't have to be at levels set by hotels and attractions with massive ad spends and influencers who are paid small fortunes to get you to buy into something you could have for a fraction of the cost.

This book is for those who want to have the cold hard budget busting facts to hand (which is why we've included so many one page charts, which you can use as a quick reference), but otherwise, the book provides plenty of tips to help you shape your own Adelaide experience.

We have designed this travel guide to give you a unique planning tool to experience an unforgettable trip without spending the ascribed tourist budget.

This guide focuses on Adelaide's unbelievable bargains. Of course, there is little value in traveling to Adelaide and not experiencing everything it has to offer. Where possible, we've included cheap workarounds or listed the experience in the Loved but Costly section.

When it comes to FUN budget travel, it's all about what you know. You can have all the feels without most of the bills. A few days spent planning can save you thousands. Luckily, we've done the planning for you, so you can distill the information in minutes not days, leaving you to focus on what matters: immersing yourself in the sights, sounds and smells of Adelaide, meeting awesome new people and feeling relaxed and happy. I sincerely hope our tips will bring you great joy at a fraction of the price you expected.

So, grab a cup of tea or coffee, put your feet up and relax; you're about to enter the world of enjoying Adelaide on the cheap. Oh, and don't forget a biscuit. You need energy to plan a trip of a lifetime on a budget.

# Super Cheap Adelaide is <u>not</u> for travellers with the following needs:

1. You require a book with detailed offline travel maps. Super Cheap Insider Guides are best used with Google Maps - download before you travel to make the most of your time and money.
2. You would like thousands of accommodation, food and attraction recommendations; by definition, cheapest is often singular. We only include maximum value recommendations. We purposively leave out over-priced attractions when there is no workaround.
3. You would like detailed write-ups about hotels/ Airbnbs/Restaurants. We are bargain hunters first and foremost. We dedicate our time to finding the best deals, not writing flowery language about their interiors. Plus, things change. If I had a pound for every time I'd read a Lonely Planet description only to find the place totally different, I would be a rich man. Always look at online reviews for the latest up-to-date information.

If you want to save A LOT of money while comfortably enjoying an unforgettable trip to Adelaide, minus the marketing, hype, scams and tourist traps read on.

# Discover Adelaide

*Moana beach*

Adelaide is a sophisticated, breathable, cosmopolitan city that is all about the finer things in life, but that doesn't mean they come with a big price tag. Here you can enjoy fine wine, finer food, fine beaches and fine people for a snip - as they say in Aussie - the name given to Australian slang.

Adelaide is home to 1.3 million people. I met many Adelaidean's who were keen to tell me no convicts were sent here! Count how many people tell you this - I bet it surpasses 10.

Adelaide was named after the wife of British king William IV. it has a liberal history as the first state to decriminalise homosexuality and legalise abortion. Women stood as MP's here from 1894.

**History**

Home to many indigenous tribes for thousands of years before European settlement began in 1836, Adelaide has since welcomed migrants from all over the world and is characterised by a great diversity of cultural traditions, languages spoken and systems of belief. The state of South Australia boasts a stable economy and low unemployment rate, with a broad base of thriving industries, including agriculture, wine, information and communications technology, automotive production, defence, biosciences, health, tourism and the arts.

## Festivals

The city hosts many festivals, including WOMADelaide, the Adelaide, Festival of Arts and the Adelaide Fringe Festival, and has an extensive range of world-class sporting and recreational facilities. Known as the 20-minute city, Adelaide is easy to get around thanks to its broad boulevards and public transport network. Its central location makes it an ideal gateway to explore South Australia's many tourist attractions, from world-renowned wineries and rugged coastlines to the Australian outback.

## Cuisine

Adelaides love their food. Over 100 fine dining restaurants exist alongside pop-up restaurants and food trucks. Adelaide is the wine capital of Australia, with well known brands such as Jacobs Creek growing their grapes nearby. There is no other city in the country which offers you such easy access to the vineyards. The Barossa Valley and Adelaide Hills are a short distance from the city.

## Adelaide People

Adelaide is the city which is not just known for its heart stealing climate and natural beauty, but also for the people who are cherish helping others all the time. This picturesque city is full of amicable people who will go out of their way to help you. You will see a lot of Indian people, many Sikh, as well as women wearing the hijab. There is also a strong Italian community.

## How to make friends with the locals

It's not a city known for its night-life or party scene, but you will not struggle to strike up a conversation in and around the green space where flocks of parrots are in the trees. You can get around happily and inexpensively on public transport where people can often be seen striking up a conversation. It's a relaxing city that moves at a pace that will not age you quickly or generally make you weary over time so take the same approach to making friends with the locals.

Adelaide can be a budget-buster, but take heart. The trick to keeping your trip affordable is to get off the tourist track and find the local deals. Use this guide to make sure Adelaide leaves a lasting impression on your heart and mind, not your bank balance.

## What's the weather like in Adelaide?
Adelaide has a welcoming climate made up of pleasant, warm summers and mild, short winters. In the hotter months, expats will find themselves with over 14 hours of sunlight, but with plenty of opportunity to find respite in the form of a beach. Most of the rain in Adelaide falls between April and October.

# Some of Adelaide's Best Bargains

# Visit the Adelaide Botanic Garden

FREE guided walks of Adelaide's Botanic Garden opened in 1857 leave from outside the Visitor Information Centre on the Schomburgk Pavilion at 10:30am daily.
More information: https://www.botanicgardens.sa.gov.au/whats-on/tours-trails

# Explore the Art gallery of South Australia

The mix of classic and contemporary art at Art gallery of South Australia is unparalleled. To understand the pieces you can take a free tour. They depart from the North Terrace entrance at 11 am and 2 pm. Tours depart from the North Terrace entrance.

# Marvel at State Library of South Australia

Adelaide's state library took over 18 years to complete. The craftsmanship and engineering is awe-inspiring. Opened on 18 December 1884 the Adelaide library holds a lot of local secrets. You can take a free tour from Monday to Friday at 11 am and 2 pm. They depart from the upper floor adjacent to the Cloakroom.

# Take a tour of Parliament House

Women were granted the right to vote here in 1894, the first place in the world to do so after New Zealand! Entry to the Parliament is free, with doors open from 9:00am to 5:00pm Monday to Friday. Free tours run at 10 am and 2 pm on weekdays subject to availability.

# Do Adelaide Fringe on the cheap

The world's second-largest annual arts festival, Adelaide Fringe is taking place from 17 February - 19 March 2023.

Adelaide Fringe is offering two memberships to get people back to events.

"Fringe Membership Fanatic ($40) unlocks 2for1 tickets to all participating FM Fringe 2023 shows and loads more.

Fringe Membership ($29) express ticketing collect and 5x 2for1 tix to participating FM Fringe 2023 shows.

You join 7,000+ entertainment lovers in Adelaide and unlock secret events, free movie screenings and exclusive discounts all year round. Membership is valid for one year from the date of purchase."

More information is available here: adelaidefringe.com.au/fringe-membership

The next 10 pages contain psychological hacks for saving money in Adelaide. If you are only interested in the tangible tips skip to How to Feel Rich in Adelaide.

# How to Enjoy ALLOCATING Money in Adelaide

**'Money's greatest intrinsic value—and this can't be overstated—is its ability to give you control over your time.' - Morgan Housel**

Notice I have titled the chapter how to enjoy allocating money in Adelaide. I'll use saving and allocating interchangeably in the book, but since most people associate saving to feel like a turtleneck, that's too tight, I've chosen to use wealth language. Rich people don't save. They allocate. What's the difference? Saving can feel like something you don't want or wish to do and allocating has your personal will attached to it.

And on that note, it would be helpful if you considered removing the following words and phrase from your vocabulary for planning and enjoying your Adelaide trip:

- Wish

- Want

- Maybe someday

These words are part of poverty language. Language is a dominant source of creation. Use it to your advantage. You don't have to wish, want or say maybe someday to Adelaide. You can enjoy the same things millionaires enjoy in Adelaide without the huge spend.

**'People don't like to be sold-but they love to buy.' - Jeffrey Gitomer**.

Every good salesperson who understands the quote above places obstacles in the way of their clients' buying. Companies create waiting lists, restaurants pay people to queue outside in order to create demand. People reason if something is so in demand, it must be worth having but that's often just marketing. Take this sales maxim 'People don't like to be sold-but they love to buy and flip it on its head to allocate your money in Adelaide on things YOU desire. You love to spend and hate to be sold. That means when something comes your way, it's not 'I can't afford it,' it's 'I don't want it' or maybe 'I don't want it right now'.

Saving money doesn't mean never buying a latte, never taking a taxi, never taking vacations (of course, you bought this book). Only you get to decide on how you spend and on what. Not an advice columnist who thinks you can buy a house if you never eat avocado toast again.

I love what Kate Northrup says about affording something: "If you really wanted it you would figure out a way to get it. If it were that VALUABLE to you, you would make it happen."

I believe if you master the art of allocating money to bargains, it can feel even better than spending it! Bold claim, I know. But here's the truth: Money gives you freedom and options. The more you keep in your account and or invested the more freedom and options you'll have. The principal reason you should save and allocate money is TO BE FREE! Remember, a trip's main purpose is relaxation, rest and enjoyment, aka to feel free.

When you talk to most people about saving money on vacation. They grimace. How awful they proclaim not to go wild on your vacation. If you can't get into a ton of debt enjoying your once-in-a-lifetime vacation, when can you?

When you spend money 'theres's a sudden rush of dopamine which vanishes once the transaction is complete. What happens in the brain when you save money? It increases feelings of security and peace. You don't need to stress life's uncertainties. And having a greater sense of peace can actually help you save more money.' Stressed out people make impulsive financial choices, calm people don't.'

The secret to enjoying saving money on vacation is very simple: never save money from a position of lack. Don't think 'I wish I could afford that'. Choose not to be marketed to. Choose not to consume at a price others set. Don't save money from the flawed premise you don't have enough. Don't waste your time living in the box that society has created, which says saving money on vacation means sacrifice. It doesn't.

Traveling to Adelaide can be an expensive endeavor if you don't approach it with a plan, but you have this book which is packed with tips. The biggest other asset is your perspective.

## Money is an illusion

There are 180 different currencies in the world today. And incredibly, only 8% of it is actual, physical, hold-it-in-your-hand cash. Just take a moment to really think about that. 92% of all money is merely numbers. Numbers on a screen. Nothing more.

Money was invented as an efficient way for us to transact with each other. Can you imagine how laborious it would be if to buy fruits and vegetables you had to find someone who wanted the stunning oil painting you just finished. Most people would die of starvation before interests were married up. Money is efficient. Any other attribute you attach to it is just what society has told you. Money is neither good nor bad. It is merely numbers making life efficient. Different people attach different numbers, but you can always find a number that suits you.

## A simple exercise to Face Your Money Blocks

Many of us hold limiting money beliefs, which stops money flowing to and from us. Money blocks come from everything around you: parents, teachers, news, movies and even music. I overcame mine with a very simple technique. Take a piece of paper. Fold it in two. On one side, write your top three beliefs about money. For illustrative purposes, here were mine:

1. I do not deserve money (doesn't everyone have that one?)

2. I am 'no-good' with money.

3. Money is evil

Then turn the paper over and write your beliefs out to be the exact opposite. Again here are mine:

1. I deserve money

2. I am great with money. I use it to help myself and others. My money lifts people up.

3. Money is good.

Now keep this new list on you and set an alarm to look at it three times a day. That's it.

I did this several years ago and experienced a complete financial turnaround. You can literally see it in my book listings on Amazon. It works.

## Enjoy spending money

Erm? I thought this was all about saving money? Yes, yes, it is, but to do that, you must really, truly enjoy spending money. You spent money buying this book. By buying this book, you have clothed and fed my baby (5 months old) and my toddler (a rambunctious 2 and a half year old). If every-time you spent money you thought about the people it's helping, you would feel pretty darn good about spending it. You must absolutely enjoy spending money to be a wise allocator.

Warren Buffet is famous for driving an old car and not buying his daughter a new kitchen, but yet he brilliantly allocates billions in companies and philanthropic endeavors. Despite the doom and gloom headlines about inflation and war in Ukraine, money is everywhere and you can enjoy spending and allocating your money.

Truth be told, I have been struggling to write this part of the book for two solid weeks. I have written it. Rewritten it. Started over completely from scratch. And on and on. It turns out there was something I needed to do.

Finding bargains and giving generously give me a drug like high that I can explain in no other words than to say: I feel pure ecstasy. It's as if sun flares are beaming off my skin. In fact, there's only one thing I spend on where I don't look for bargains - random acts of kindness. I should make the point, my random acts of kindness are completely selfish. When I do one, I normally receive a pleasant surprise. Like the adage goes, the more we give, the more we receive. Recently I cut out my random acts of kindness, partly because my gas and electricity bills have quadrupled and partly because I've imbibed too much doom and gloom inflation news.

'Researchers from Carnegie Mellon University, Stanford University, and MIT Sloan studied MRI images of people's brains as they made financial decisions. What they discovered is that the nucleus accumbens -- the "feel good" center of the brain -- lights up when people contemplate a purchase. When those same people think about how much a specific purchase is going to cost, it is the insula -- a tucked-away part of the brain described as the "seat of disgust and pain" -- that lights up.'

The entire purpose of this book is to stop your insula from lighting up. Saving and or allocating money doesn't mean not spending it. It means spending it on things you truly desire at levels that create a feeling of security for you.

This morning I put some money in a woman's postbox. I've never really spoken to this woman. Once it was raining and she went out of her way to offer me an umbrella when I was wearing my newborn. Months before I even conceived this part of the book, someone told me she was having chemo for breast cancer. I told the person who told me to give her my best, and I said a prayer for her. Then I totally forgot about it. Not on purpose, but just in the way the practicalities of work, kids, wives override other people's problems. I was walking my dog wondering why on earth I can't finish this part of the book when I asked myself the question: what's the best money I can spend today?

Where was I? Outside her house. I imagined her returning from a chemo session and finding a pleasant surprise. The feeling enveloped me in such a beautiful heat. I stopped in my tracks, took out some money and put it in her mailbox. I walked away grinning ear to ear. This random act of kindness was key to me finishing this work. I will enjoy thinking of her smile when she finds the money in her mailbox for many, many years. That feeling is definitely worth much more to me than the money I parted with, so it was the best money I could spend today. The take away is this: If you're going to experience a warm glow of pure unadulterated happiness from spending the money, be it on a latte, avocado toast, a skydive over Adelaide or just putting money in someone's postbox, spend the money. If it's really the best money you can spend today, spend it. And lap up every rush of happiness it brings you.

I'm not advocating an altruistic approach to spending money. You, more than anyone, deserve your love and compassion, and that means investing in yourself. If a latte is going to get you buzzing, then enjoy allocating money to one.

My point here's always a way to allocate money to the things you truly desire. This book will show you how not to let the posted cost of something make you believe you can't have it.

# Common pitfalls when it comes to allocating money to <u>your desires</u> while traveling

### Beware of Malleable mental accounting

Let's say you budgeted spending only $30 per day in Adelaide but then you say well if I was at home I'd be spending $30 on food as an everyday purchase so you add another $30 to your budget. Don't fall into that trap as the likelihood is you still have expenses at home even if its just the cost of keeping your freezer going.

### Beware of impulse purchases in Adelaide

Restaurants that you haven't researched and just idle into can sometimes turn out to be great, but more often, they turn out to suck, especially if they are near tourist attractions. Make yourself a travel itinerary including where you'll eat breakfast and lunch. Dinner is always more expensive, so the meal best to enjoy at home or as a takeaway. This book is full of incredible cheap eats. All you have to do is plan to go to them.

### Social media and FOMO (Fear of Missing Out)

'The pull of seeing acquaintances spend money on travel can often be a more powerful motivator to spend more while traveling than seeing an advertisement.' Beware of what you allow to influence you and go back to the question, what's the best money I can spend today?

## Now-or-never sales strategies

One reason tourists are targeted by salespeople is the success of the now-or-never strategy. If you don't spend the money now… your never get the opportunity again. Rarely is this true.

Instead of spending your money on something you might not actually desire, take five minutes. Ask yourself, do I really want this? And return to the answer in five minutes. Your body will either say an absolute yes with a warm, excited feeling or a no with a weak, obscure feeling.

## Unexpected costs

**"Holding on to anger is like grasping a hot coal with the intent of throwing it at someone else; you only hurt yourself." The Buddha.**

One downside to traveling is unexpected costs. When these spring up from airlines, accommodation providers, tours and on and on, they feel like a punch in the gut. During the pandemic my earnings fell to 20% of what they are normally. No one was traveling, no one was buying travel guides. My accountant out of nowhere significantly raised his fee for the year despite the fact there was a lot less money to count. I was so angry I consulted a lawyer who told me you will spend more taking him to court than you will paying his bill. I had to get myself into a good feeling place before I paid his bill, so I googled how to feel good paying someone who has scammed you.

The answer: Write down that you will receive 10 times the amount you are paying from an unexpected source. I did that. Four months later, the accountant wrote to me. He had applied for a COVID subsidy for me and I would receive… you guessed it almost exactly 10 times his fee.

Make of that what you want. I don't wish to get embroiled in a conversation about what many term 'woo-woo', but the result of my writing that I would receive 10 times the amount made me feel much, much better when paying him. And ultimately, that was a gift in itself. So next time some airline or train operator or hotel/ Airbnb sticks you with an unexpected fee, immediately write that you will receive 10 times the amount you are paying from an unexpected source. Rise your vibe and skip the added price of feeling angry.

# Hack your allocations for your Adelaide Trip

**"The best trick for saving is to eliminate the decision to save." Perry Wright of Duke University.**

Put the money you plan to spend in Adelaide on a pre-paid card in the local currency. This cuts out two problems - not knowing how much you've spent and totally avoiding expensive currency conversion fees.

You could even create separate spaces. This much for transportation, this for tours/entertainment, accommodation and food. We are reluctant to spend money that is pre-assigned to categories or uses.

Write that you want to enjoy a $3,000 trip for $500 to your Adelaide trip. Countless research shows when you put goals in writing, you have a higher chance of following through.

**Spend all the money you want to on buying experiences in Adelaide**

**"Experiences are like good relatives that stay for a while and then leave. Objects are like relatives who move in and stay past their welcome." Daniel Gilbert, psychologist from Harvard University.**

Economic and psychological research shows we are happier buying brief experiences on vacation rather than buying stuff to wear so give yourself freedom to spend on experiences knowing that like my random acts of kindness the value you get back is many many times over.

**Make saving money a game**

There's one day a year where all the thrift shops where me and my family live sell everything there for a $1. My wife and I hold a contest where we take $5 and buy an entire outfit for each other. Whoever's outfit is liked more wins. We also look online to see whose outfit would have cost more to buy new. This year, my wife even snagged me an Armani coat for $1. I liked the coat when she showed it to me, but when I found out it was $500 new; I liked it and wore it a lot more.

## Quadruple your money

Every-time you want to spend money, imagine it quadrupled. So the $10 you want to spend is actually $40. Now imagine that what you want to buy is four times the price. Do you still want it? If yes, go enjoy. If not, you've just saved yourself money, know you can choose to invest it in a way that quadruples or allocate it to something you really want to give you a greater return.

## Understand what having unlimited amounts of money to spend in Adelaide actually looks like

Let's look at what it would be like to have unlimited amounts of money to spend on your trip to Adelaide.

## Isolation

You take a private jet to your private Adelaide hotel. There you are lavished with the best food, drink, and entertainment. Spending vast amounts of money on vacation equals being isolated.

If you're on your honeymoon and you want to be alone with your Amore, this is wonderful, but it can be equally wonderful to make new friends. Know this a study 'carried out by Brigham Young University, Utah found that while obesity increased risk of death by 30%, loneliness increased it by half.'

## Comfort

Money can buy you late check outs of five-star hotels and priority boarding on airlines, all of which add up to comfort. But as this book will show you, saving money in Adelaide doesn't minimize comfort, that's just a lie travel agencies littered with glossy brochures want you to believe.

You can do late-check outs for free with the right credit cards and priority boarding can be purchased with a lot of airlines from $4. If you want to go big with first-class or business, flights offset your own travel costs by renting your own home or you can upgrade at the airport often for a fraction of what you would have paid booking a business flight online.

# How to feel RICH in Adelaide

Contrary to what advertisers want you to believe, you don't need millions in your bank to **feel rich**. Feeling rich feels different to every person. For me, it's the health and safety of my children and wife and the freedom to travel. For you, it might be something completely different.

"Researchers have pooled data on the relationship between money and emotions from more than 1.6 million people across 162 countries and found that **wealthier people feel more positive "self-regard emotions" such as confidence, pride and determination.**"

Regardless of what feeling rich feels like to you, we can all agree it feels good. Here are things to see, do and taste in Adelaide, that will have you overflowing with gratitude for your luxury trip to Adelaide.

• Achieving a Michelin Star rating is the most coveted accolade for restaurants but those that obtain a Michelin Star are synonymous with high cost, but in Adelaide there are restaurants with Michelin-stars offering lunch menus for 30 dollars or less!If you want to taste the finest seasonal local dishes while dining in pure luxury, visit **Tim Ho Wan**, to indulge in an unforgettable treat. If fine dining isn't your thing, don't worry further on in the guide you will find a range of delicious cheap eats in Adelaide that deserve a Michelin-Star.

• While money can't buy happiness, it can buy cake and isn't that sort of the same thing? Jokes aside, Bakery on O'Connell in Adelaide have turned cakes and pastries into edible art. Visit to taste the most delicious croissant in Adelaide.

- While you might not be staying in a penthouse, you can still enjoy the same views. Visit rooftop bars in Adelaide, like Sôl Bar & Restaurant to enjoy incredible sunset views for the price of just one drink. And if you want to continue enjoying libations, head over to Lady Burra for a dirt-cheap happy hour, lots of reasonably priced (and delicious) cocktails and cheap delicious snacks.

Those are just some ideas for you to know that visiting Adelaide on a budget doesn't have to feel like sacrifice or constriction. Now let's get into the nuts and bolts of Adelaide on the super cheap.

# Redefining Super Cheap

The value you get out of Super Cheap Adelaide is not based on what you paid for it; it's based on what you do with it. You can only do great things with it if you believe saving money is worth your time. Charging things to your credit card and thinking 'oh I'll pay it off when I get home' is something you won't be tempted to do if you change your beliefs now. Think about what you associate with the word cheap, because you make your beliefs and your beliefs make you.

I grew up thinking you had to spend more than you could afford to have a good time traveling. Now I've visited 190 countries, I know nothing is further from the truth. Before you embark upon reading our specific tips for Adelaide think about your associations with the word cheap.

Here are the dictionary definitions of cheap:

- Costing very little; relatively low in price; inexpensive: a cheap dress.
- costing little labor or trouble: Words are cheap.
- charging low prices: a very cheap store.
- Of little account; of small value; mean; shoddy: Cheap conduct; cheap workmanship.
- Embarrassed; sheepish: He felt cheap about his mistake.
- Stingy; miserly: He's too cheap to buy his own brother a cup of coffee.

Three out of six definitions have extremely negative connotations. The 'super cheap' we're talking about in this book is not shoddy, embarrassed, or stingy.
We added the super to reinforce our message. Super's dictionary definition stands for 'a super quality'. Super Cheap stands for enjoying the best on the lowest budget. Question other people's definitions of cheap so you're not blinded to possibilities, poten-

tial, and prosperity. Here are some new associations to consider forging:

## Shoddy

Cheap stuff doesn't last is an adage marketing companies have drilled into consumers. However, by asking vendors the right questions cheap doesn't mean something won't last. I had a $10 backpack last for 8 years and a $100 suitcase bust on the first journey.

A study out of San Francisco University found that people who spent money on experiences rather than things were happier. Memories last forever, not things, even expensive things. And as we will show you during this guide, you don't need to pay to create glorious memories.[1]

## Embarrassed

I have friends who routinely pay more to vendors because they think their money is putting food on this person's table. Paradoxically, Cuban doctors are driving taxis because they earn more money; it's not always a good thing for the place you're visiting to pay more and can cause unwanted distortion in their culture - Airbnb pushing out renters is an obvious example. Think carefully about whether the extra money is helping people or incentivising greed.

## Stingy

Cheap can be eco-friendly. Buying

---

[1]      Paulina Pchelin & Ryan T. Howell (2014) The hidden cost of value-seeking: People do not accurately forecast the economic benefits of experiential purchases, The Journal of Positive Psychology, 9:4, 322-334, DOI: 10.1080/17439760.2014.898316

clothes is cheap, but you also help the Earth. Many travellers are often disillusioned by the reality of traveling since the places on our bucket-lists are overcrowded. Cheap can take you away from the crowds.  You can find balance and harmony being cheap. "Remember a journey is best measured in friends, rather than miles." – Tim Cahill. And making friends is free!

A recent survey by Credit Karma found 50% of Millennials and Gen Z get into debt traveling. **Please don't allow credit card debt to be an unwanted souvenir you take home.** As you will see from this book, there's so much you can enjoy in Adelaide for free, some many unique bargains and so many ways to save money! You just need to want to!

# Planning your trip

## The best time to visit

The first step in saving money on your Adelaide trip is timing. Visit from June to August or March to May or September. Rainfall is rare and daytime temperatures sit in the 60s and 70s and prices are lowest.

## Visit Adelaide on your birthday

Companies know rewarding customers on their birthdays will boost retention so many in Adelaide go out of their way to surprise customers and make them feel special on their birthdays. Visit Adelaide on your birthday you can get well over $150 of free meals, cakes and more. All you need is a valid ID to claim your birthday gifts at:

- San Churro
- Boost Juice
- Muffin Break
- Nandos
- Oporto
- Baskin Robbins
- Salsa's
- Jamaica Blue.

Here is a regularly updated list of Adelaide Birthday freebies: https://www.finder.com.au/free-stuff-on-birthday-australia

# Stay in Airbnb

Airbnb's here are 70% cheaper than hotels. If you want to stay in hostels, we found the best value. You can find a private room in the city for less than $20 or an entire apartment a bit further out for a similar price.

It can be expensive to eat out so book an Airbnb and cook some of your meals at home. You can buy great fresh produce from The Central market, Aldi or NQR.

## Where to stay

Adelaide is an easy city to get around, so stay where you find the best Airbnb to suit your needs. Here are the main attractions:

### North Terrace
Adelaide's cultural heart, with the SA Museum, Art Gallery of SA, State Library, Adelaide University and the Botanic Garden .

**Rundle Mall**
with over 800 stores to choose from, Rundle Mall is Adelaide's vibrant retail heart.
**Central Market**
the fresh produce heart of Adelaide, offering an amazing selection of fresh produce.
**Rundle Street East**
with a great selection of restaurants and bars only a few steps from a 99C bus stop.
**Gouger Street**
Adelaide's greatest selection of restaurants catering for all budgets and tastes and  just a short walk from either free tram or bus stops

## AVOID The weekend price hike in peak season

Hostel and hotel prices skyrocket during weekends in peak season. If you can get out of Adelaide for the weekend if you visit in the peak season you'll save $$$ on your accommodation. For example a dorm room at a popular Hostel costs $44 a night during the week. That price goes to $253 for Saturday's and Sundays.

# Get Free meals and Accommodation

If you want a taste of the real-life in Australia you can help farmers with harvesting. You'll get to interact with local farmers, pet the farm animals and unwind in the relaxing rural atmosphere while receiving a free stay and meals in exchange for helping.

If you're interested check out Downunder Farmstays, Farmstay Planet or Workaway - www.workaway.info/en/hostlist/oceania/au?region=south-australia

# Hack your Adelaide Accommodation

Your two biggest expenses when travelling to Adelaide are accommodation and food. This section is intended to help you cut these costs dramatically before and while you are in Adelaide.

Hostels are the cheapest accommodation in Adelaide but there are some creative workarounds to upgrade your stay on the cheap.

### Use Time

There are two ways to use time. One is to book in advance. Three months will net you the best deal, especially if your visit coincides with an event. The other is to book on the day of your stay. This is a risky move, but if executed well, you can lay your head in a five-star hotel for a 2-star fee.

Before I travelled to Adelaide, I checked for big events using a simple google search 'What's on in Adelaide', there were no big events drawing travellers so I risked showing up with no accommodation booked (If there are big events on demand exceeds supply and you should avoid using this strategy) I started checking for discount rooms at 11 am using a private browser on booking.com.

Before I go into demand-based pricing, take a moment to think about your risk tolerance. By risk, I am not talking about personal safety. No amount of financial savings is worth risking that. What I am talking about is being inconvenienced. Do you deal well with last-minute changes? Can you roll with the punches or do you dislike it if something changes? Everyone is different and knowing yourself is the best way to plan a great trip. If you are someone that likes to have everything pre-planned using demand-based pricing to get cheap accommodation will not work for you. Skip this section and go to blind-booking.

## Demand-based pricing

Be they an Airbnb host or hotel manager; no one wants empty rooms. Most will do anything to make some revenue because they still have the same costs to cover whether the room is occupied or not. That's why you will find many hotels drastically slashing room rates for same-day bookings.

## How to book five-star hotels for a two-star price

You will not be able to find these discounts when the demand exceeds the supply. So if you're visiting during the peak season, or during an event which has drawn many travellers don't try this.

On the day of your stay, visit booking.com (which offers better discounts than Kayak and agoda.com). Hotel Tonight individually checks for any last-minute bookings, but they take a big chunk of the action, so the better deals come from booking.com. The best results come from booking between 2 pm and 4 pm when the risk of losing any revenue with no occupancy is most pronounced, so algorithms supporting hotels slash prices. This is when you can find rates that are not within the "lowest publicly visible" rate. To avoid losing customers to other websites, or cheapening the image of their hotel most will only offer the super cheap rates during a two hour window from 2 pm to 4 pm. Two guests will pay 10x difference in price but it's absolutely vital to the hotel that neither knows it.

**Takeaway**: To get the lowest price book on the day of stay between 2 pm and 4 pm and extend your search radius to include further afield hotels with good transport connections.

# Priceline Hack to get a Luxury Hotel on the Cheap

Priceline.com has been around since 1997 and is an incredible site for sourcing luxury Hotels on the cheap in Adelaide. If you've tried everything else and that's failed, priceline will deliver.

Priceline have a database of the lowest price a hotel will accept for a particular time and date. That amount changes depending on two factors:

1. Demand: More demand high prices.
2. Likelihood of lost revenue: if the room is still available at 3pm the same-day prices will plummet.

Obviously they don't want you to know the lowest price as they make more commission the higher the price you pay.

They offer two good deals to entice you to book with them in Adelaide. And the good news is neither require last-minute booking (though the price will decrease the closer to the date you book).

'Firstly, 'price-breakers'. You blind book from a choice of three highly rated hotels which they name. Pricebreakers, travelers are shown three similar, highly-rated hotels, listed under a single low price.' After you book they reveal the name of the hotel.

Secondly, the 'express deals'. These are the last minute deals. You'll be able to see the name of the hotel before you book.

To find the right luxury hotel for you at a cheap price you should plug in the
neighbourhoods you want to stay in, an acceptable rating (4 or 5 stars), and filter by the amenities you want.

You can also get an addition discount for your Adelaide hotel by booking on their dedicated app.

**How to trick travel Algorithms to get the lowest hotel price**

Do not believe anyone who says changing your IP address to get cheaper hotels or flights does NOT work. If you don't believe us, download a Tor Network and search for flights and hotels to one destination using your current IP and then the tor network (a tor browser hides your IP address from algorithms. It is commonly used by hackers). You will receive different prices.

The price you see is a decision made by an algorithm that adjusts prices using data points such as past bookings, remaining capacity, average demand and the probability of selling the room or flight later at a higher price. If knows you've searched for the area before ip the prices high. To circumvent this, you can either use a different IP address from a cafe or airport or data from an international sim. I use a sim from Three, which provides free data in many countries around the world. When you search from a new IP address, most of the time, and particularly near booking you will get a lower price. Sometimes if your sim comes from a 'rich' country, say the UK or USA, you will see higher rates as the algorithm has learnt people from these countries pay more. The solution is to book from a local wifi connection - but a different one from the one you originally searched from.

## How to get last-minute discounts on owner rented properties

In addition to Airbnb, you can also find owner rented rooms and apartments on www.vrbo.com or HomeAway or a host of others.

Nearly all owners renting accommodation will happily give renters a "last-minute" discount to avoid the space sitting empty, not earning a dime.

Go to Airbnb or another platform and put in today's date. Once you've found something you like start the negotiating by asking for a 25% reduction. A sample message to an Airbnb host might read:

Dear HOST NAME,

I love your apartment. It looks perfect for me. Unfortunately, I'm on a very tight budget. I hope you won't be offended, but I wanted to ask if you would be amenable to offering me a 25% discount for tonight, tomorrow and the following day? I see that you aren't booked. I can assure you, I will leave your place exactly the way I found it. I will put bed linen in the washer and ensure everything is clean for the next guest. I would be delighted to bring you a bottle of wine to thank you for any discount that you could offer.

If this sounds okay, please send me a custom offer, and I will book straight away.

YOUR NAME.

In my experience, a polite, genuine message like this, that proposes reciprocity will be successful 80% of the time. Don't ask for more than 25% off, this person still has to pay the bills and will probably say no as your stay will cost them more in bills than they make. Plus starting higher, can offend the owner and do you want to stay somewhere, where you have offended the host?

### In Practice
To use either of these methods, you must travel light. Less stuff means greater mobility, everything is faster and you don't have to

check-in or store luggage. If you have a lot of luggage, you're going to have fewer of these opportunities to save on accommodation. Plus travelling light benefits the planet - you're buying, consuming, and transporting less stuff.

## Blind-booking

If your risk tolerance does not allow for last-minute booking, you can use blind-booking. Many hotels not wanting to cheapen their brand with known low-prices, choose to operate a blind booking policy. This is where you book without knowing the name of the hotel you're going to stay in until you've made the payment. This is also sometimes used as a marketing strategy where the hotel is seeking to recover from past issues. I've stayed in plenty of blind book hotels. As long as you choose 4 or 5 star hotels, you will find them to be clean, comfortable and safe. priceline.com, Hot Rate® Hotels and Top Secret Hotels (operated by last-minute.com) offer the best deals.

## Hotels.com Loyalty Program

This is currently the best hotel loyalty program with hotels in Adelaide. The basic premise is you collect 10 nights and get 1 free. hotels.com price match, so if booking.com has a cheaper price you can get hotel.com, to match. If you intend to travel more than ten nights in a year, its a great choice to get the 11th free.


## Don't let time use you.

Rigidity will cost you money. You pay the price you're willing to pay, not the amount it  requires a hotel to deliver. Therefore if you're in town for a big event, saving money on accommodation is nearly impossible so in such cases book three months ahead.

# The best price performance location in Adelaide

A room putting Adelaide's local attractions, restaurants, and nightlife are within walking distance will save you time on transport. Restaurants and bars don't get that much cheaper the further you go from famous tourist attractions. But you will also get a better idea of the day to day life of a local if you stay in a neighbourhood like Elizabeth. It depends on the Adelaide you want to experience. For the tourist experience stay in the centre either in a last-minute hotel or Airbnb. For a taste of local life the leafy district of Elizabeth is the best you will find. Adelaide Riviera Hotel is a luxurious hotel with consistent last-minute rooms from $30 a night.

## What to do if you only find overpriced options

If when you're searching for accommodation, you can only find overpriced offers, it's likely that you're visiting at a time where demand outstrips supply. In this case, have a look at www.trustedhousesitters.com. You stay for free when you care for someones pets. If you really can't find a good deal, this can be worth doing but only you know if you want to make a commitment to care for someone else's pets while on vacation. Some find it relaxing, others don't. The properties in Adelaide can be even more stunning than five-star hotels but if you're new to house sitting you might be against 10+ applicants, so make sure your profile is really strong before you apply for a sit. It could save you a small fortune and, who knows, you could even make some new (furry and non-furry) friends.

# Saving money on Adelaide Food

An oft-quoted parable is 'There is no such thing as cheap food. Either you pay at the cash registry or the doctor's office'. This dismisses the fact that good nutrition is a choice; we all make every-time we eat. Cheap eats are not confined to hotdogs and kebabs. In Adelaide you can eat nutritious food cheaply.

Japan has the longest life expectancy in the world. A national study by the Japanese Ministry of Internal Affairs and Communications revealed that between January and May 2019, a household of two spent on average ¥65,994 a month, that's $10 per person per day on food. You truly don't need to spend a lot to eat nutritious food in Adelaide. That's a marketing gimmick hawkers of overpriced muesli bars want you to believe.

**Eat at Food trucks**
Grab a cheap bite on the go from Adelaide's best food trucks: Moorish Bites Food Truck, Moroccan, Mum and Meloui, Manufacture a Great Moment and Veggie Velo Food Truck - Good wholesome and delicious veggie burgers.

**Eat at bakeries**
Cannelle French Pastries and Bakery on O'Connell offer excellent and several healthy baked goods.

**Enjoy Cheap Nutritious Breakfasts in Adelaide**
If you stay somewhere with a free breakfast, eat smart. Don't eat sugary cereals or white flour rich pastries if you don't want to be hungry an hour later. Before leaving your hotel or checking out, find some fresh fruit, water, and granola in the fitness centre or coffee in the lobby or business centre.  If your hotel doesn't have free breakfast, don't take it. You can always eat cheaper outside.

Big Table has the best cheap breakfast we found in Adelaide.

**Visit supermarkets at discount times.**
You can get a 50 per cent discount around 5 pm at the Coles and Woolworths supermarkets on fresh produce. The cheaper the supermarket, the less discounts you will find, so check Coles and Woolworths at 5 pm before heading to discount retailer Aldi for your main shop.

NQR is an Australian discount supermarket that offers savings of up to 80% RRP on brands.

Some items at Coles and Woolworths also marked down due to sell-by date after the lunchtime rush so its also worth to check in around 3 pm.

**Use delivery services on the cheap.**
Take advantage of local offers on food delivery services. Most platforms including Menulog offer $10 off the first order in Adelaide.

**Take advantage of happy hours**

Happy hour drinks are a serious local pastime indulged in from 5pm to 7pm everyday. You find the best offers at:

Crown & Anchor Hotel
Address: 196 Grenfell St

Jack & Jill's Bar and Restaurant
Address: 121 Pirie St

Exeter Hotel
Address: 246 Rundle St

The Adelaide Casino
Address: North Terrace, near the railway station

The Elephant British Pub happy hour covers most drinks including cocktails from $5.

**Is the tap water drinkable?**
Yes, refill around your water bottle at stations around the city

# SNAPSHOT: How to enjoy a $2,000 trip to Adelaide for $200

| | |
|---|---|
| Stay | Travelling in peak season:<br><br>1. Last-minute hotels via priceline.com express deals<br>2. Stay in a private room in a Airbnb if you want privacy and cooking facilities.<br>3. Stay in hostels if you want to meet over travellers.<br>4. Housesit.<br><br>Travelling in low season<br><br>1. Last minute five-star hotels.<br>2. private room close to the city - www.airbnb.com/rooms/21152790 |
| Eat | You don't need to spend a fortune in Adelaide to eat memorable food. Average meal cost: $6 - $10 |
| Move | Use free bikes/ buses. Long distance buses comes in around $40. Look at relocation campers/cars if you are travelling as couple or group to travel for free (more below). |
| See | Botanical gardens, guided free tours of state institution's. Beaches, churches, free live music and tour a vineyard. |
| Total | US$200 |

# Unique bargains we love in Adelaide

Beautiful beaches, historical towns, peculiar villages on hilltops, and abundant wildlife make Adelaide a stunning landscape to explore for free. In amongst this wealthy wine capital you'll find free bikes, bottomless coffees from Hungry Jacks and incredible bakeries. You'll love cycling everywhere because the city is flat, and you even take the bike on trains for free.

# How to use this book

Google and TripAdvisor are your on-the-go guides while travel-ing, a travel guide adds the most value during the planning phase, and if you're without Wi-Fi. Always download the google map for your destination - having an offline map will make using this guide much more comfortable. For ease of use, we've set the book out the way you travel, booking your flights, arriving, how to get around, then on to the money-saving tips. The tips we or-dered according to when you need to know the tip to save mon-ey, so free tours and combination tickets feature first. We priori-tized the rest of the tips by how much money you can save and then by how likely it was that you could find the tip with a google search. Meaning those we think you could find alone are nearer the bottom. I hope you find this layout useful. If you have any ideas about making Super Cheap Insider Guides easier to use, please email me philgattang@gmail.com

**A quick note on How We Source Super Cheap Tips**
We focus entirely on finding the best bargains. We give each of our collaborators $2,000 to hunt down never-before-seen deals. The type you either only know if you're local or by on the ground research. We spend zero on marketing and a little on designing an excellent cover. We do this yearly, which means we just keep finding more amazing ways for you to have the same experience for less, but that's also why if you read more of our guides, you may find the sentence structure familiar. Like many other guide book companies (Lonely Planet, Rough Guides, Fodor etc) we use a content management system (i.e., we repurpose some text). If that annoys you - please accept our advanced apologies its how we keep costs down.

Now let's get started with juicing the most pleasure from your trip to Adelaide with the least possible money!

# OUR SUPER CHEAP TIPS...

**Here are our specific tips for enjoying a $2,000 trip to Adelaide for $200**

# How to Find Super Cheap Flights to Adelaide

Luck is just an illusion. Anyone can find incredible flight deals. If you can be flexible you can save huge amounts of money.

**Book your flight to Adelaide for a Tuesday or Wednesday**

Tuesdays and Wednesdays are the cheapest days of the week to fly. You can take a flight to Adelaide on a Tuesday or Wednesday for less than half the price you'd pay on a Thursday Friday, Saturday, Sunday or Monday.

**Start with Google Flights (but NEVER book through them)**

I conduct upwards of 50 flight searches a day for readers. I use google flights first when looking for flights. I put specific departure but broad destination (e.g Europe) and usually find amazing deals.

The great thing about Google Flights is you can search by class. You can pick a specific destination and it will tell you which time is cheapest in which class. Or you can put in dates and you can see which area is cheapest to travel to.

But be aware Google flights does not show the cheapest prices among the flight search engines but it does offer several advantages

1.  You can see the cheapest dates for the next 8 weeks. Other search engines will blackout over 70% of the prices.
2.  You can put in multiple airports to fly from. Just use  a common to separate in the from input.
3.  If you're flexible on where you're going Google flights can show you the cheapest destinations.
4.  You can set-up price tracking, where Google will email you when prices rise or decline.

Once you have established the cheapest dates to fly go over to skyscanner.net and put those dates in. You will find sky scanner offers the cheapest flights.

# Get Alerts when Prices to Adelaide are Lowest

Google also has a nice feature which allows you to set up an alert to email you when prices to your destination are at their lowest. So if you don't have fixed dates this feature can save you a fortune.

## Baggage add-ons

It may be cheaper and more convenient to send your luggage separately with a service like sendmybag.com Often the luggage sending fee is cheaper than what the airlines charge to check baggage. Visit Lugless.com or luggagefree.com in addition to sendmybag.com for a quotation.

## Loading times

Anyone who has attempted to find a cheap flight will know the pain of excruciating long loading times. If you encounter this issue use google flights to find the cheapest dates and then go to skyscanner.net for the lowest price.

## Always try to book direct with the airline

Once you have found the cheapest flight go direct to the airlines booking page. This is advantageous in the current COVID-19 cancellation climate, because if you need to change your flights or arrange a refund, its much easier to do so, than via a third party booking agent.

That said, sometimes the third party bookers offer cheaper deals than the airline, so you need to make the decision based on how likely you think it is that disruption will impede you making those flights.

## More flight tricks and tips

www.secretflying.com/usa-deals offers a range of deals from the USA and other countries. For example you can pick-up a round trip flight non-stop from from the east coast to johannesburg for $350 return on this site

Scott's cheap flights, you can select your home airport and get emails on deals but you pay for an annual subscription. A free workaround is to download Hopper and set search alerts for trips/price drops.

Premium service of Scott's cheap flights.
They sometime have discounted business and first class but in my experience they are few and far between.

JGOOT.com has 5 times as many choices as Scott's cheap flights.

kiwi.com allows you to be able to do radius searches so you can find cheaper flights to general areas.

**Finding Error Fares**
Travel Pirates (www.travelpirates.com) is a gold-mine for finding error deals. Subscribe to their newsletter. I recently found a reader an airfare from Montreal-Brazil for a $200 round trip (mistake fare!). Of course these error fares are always certain dates, but if you can be flexible you can save a lot of money.

Things you can do that might reduce the fare to Adelaide:--
• Use a VPN (if the booker knows you booked one-way, the return fare will go up)
• Buy your ticket in a different currency

**If all else fails…**

If you can't find a cheap flight for your dates I can find one for you. I do not charge for this nor do I send affiliate links. I'll send you a screenshot of the best options

I find as airlines attach cookies to flight links. To use this free service please review this guide and send me a screenshot of your review - with your flight hacking request. I aim to reply to you within 12 hours. If it's an urgent request mark the email URGENT in the subject line and I will endeavour to reply ASAP.

## Cheapest route from USA

Jetstar are flying to Adelaide return from $560 out of Honolulu.

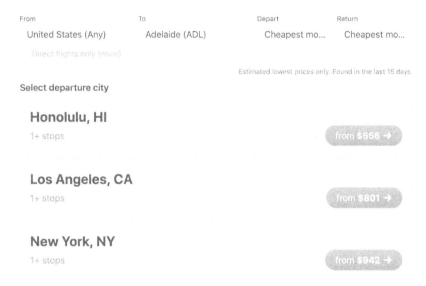

| From | To | Depart | Return |
|------|----|--------|--------|
| United States (Any) | Adelaide (ADL) | Cheapest mo... | Cheapest mo... |

Direct flights only (none)

Estimated lowest prices only. Found in the last 15 days.

Select departure city

**Honolulu, HI**
1+ stops
from $556 →

**Los Angeles, CA**
1+ stops
from $801 →

**New York, NY**
1+ stops
from $942 →

## Cheapest route from Europe

At the time of writing Qantas are flying to Adelaide from London for $690 return.

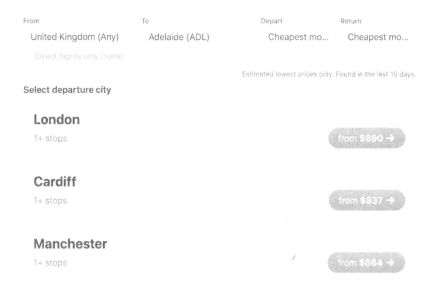

From United Kingdom (Any)    To Adelaide (ADL)    Depart Cheapest mo...    Return Cheapest mo...

Direct flights only (none)

Estimated lowest prices only. Found in the last 15 days.

**Select departure city**

### London
1+ stops

from $690 →

### Cardiff
1+ stops

from $837 →

### Manchester
1+ stops

from $864 →

# How to Find CHEAP FIRST-CLASS Flights to Adelaide

## Upgrade at the airport

Airlines are extremely reluctant to advertise price drops in first or business class tickets so the best way to secure them is at the airport when airlines have no choice but to decrease prices dramatically because otherwise they lose money. Ask about upgrading to business or first-class when you check-in. If you check-in online look around the airport for your airlines branded bidding system or go to the desk to enquire.

## Use Air-miles

When it comes to accruing air-miles for American citizens **Chase Sapphire Reserve card** ranks top. If you put everything on there and pay it off immediately you will end up getting free flights all the time, aside from taxes.

Get 2-3 chase cards with sign up bonuses, you'll have 200k points in no time and can book with points on multiple airlines when transferring your points to them.

Please note, this is only applicable to those living in the USA. In the Bonus Section we have detailed the best air-mile credit cards for those living in the UK, Canada, Germany, Austria, Spain and Australia.

### How many miles does it take to fly first class?
First class from Bangkok to Chicago (one way) costs 180,000 miles.

# Free Car and Campervan Hire Relocation

If you already have your flights booked or are in Australia, there is a free way to travel to Adelaide.

Transfercar offers free one-way rental cars and campervans. You drive for free and help rental companies relocate their cars. Rather than paying an employee to move an RV or car, companies will give you a free car or campervan as long as you're headed to the city where the campervan needs to be. To find a free car or campervan and save a small fortune on transport from or to Adelaide check out any of this relocation rental portals:

1. CoSeats.com Campervan Relocations
2. VroomVroomVroom.com.au
3. OneWayCampervans.com
4. TransferCar.com.au
5. Imoova.com
6. CheapaCampa.com.au
7. LifeSocial.com.au
8. atn.com.au
9. DriveNow.com.au
10. RVRelocations.com
11. Relocations2Go.com/au
12. HippieCamper.com
13. Transfercar.com.au
14. RelocationCarRental.com.au
15. SelfDriveShop.com
16. Reloc8it.com

# Arriving

Adelaide Airport is adjacent to West Beach, 4 miles west of the city centre. The cheapest way to the CBD is with Adelaide Metro. They operate a bus every 20 minutes. Tickets cost $4 and the journey takes 21 minutes. Take the bus from stop 10.

Taxi's are around $25 to the CBD plus a $3 levy.

**Need a place to store luggage?**

Use stasher.com to find a convenient place to store your luggage cheaply. It provides much cheaper options than airport and train station lockers in Adelaide.

# Getting around

## Rent a free bike

Adelaide has a FANTASTIC bike-sharing program, and it's free! Adelaide is a lovely city to cycle with routes out to most of the beaches and attractions. Learn more about how to take advantage of the free bikes here: bikesa.asn.au/bike-hire/adelaide-free-bikes/

**Drive** - there's an app called 'GoGet' which allows you to rent a car from $0.19 per minute + more for the Kilometre's but it's cheaper than a car rental and you can do hourly, daily or even weekly packages. You just scan the QR code on the code, hop in and drive.

# Start with this free tour

Forget exploring the city by wandering around aimlessly. Start with a free organised tour. Nothing compares to local

advice, especially when travelling on a budget. Ask for their recommendations for the best cheap eats, the best bargains, the best markets, the best place for a particular street eat. Perhaps some of it will be repeated from this guide, but it can't hurt to ask, especially if you have specific needs or questions. At the end you should leave an appropriate tip (usually around $5), but nobody bats an eye lid if you are unable or unwilling to do so, tell them you will leave a good review and always give them a little gift from home.

You can book your free walking tour here: www.tiqy.com/tour-activity-info/culture-history-free-walking-tour-around-adelaide

You can also get a free bus tour of the city by boarding the free buses numbers 98A and 98C or 99A and 99C (Adelaide Metro Free City Connector Loop Buses). These buses run from Monday to Friday

# Visit a Free museum

If you needed another reason to go to South Australian Museum it has the largest exhibition of Aboriginal Art and History!

Afterwards enjoy a free chocolate tour at nearby Haigh chocolate factory. You can book a free tour online here: https://www.haighschocolates.com.au/

# Do a wine tour on the cheap

Adelaide is one of the ten wine capitals of the world. Barossa Vally, the Adelaide Hills or McLaren Vale are just one hour from the city (opposite directions of the city though). Each wine valley is absolutely beautiful, and offers amazing wine. You need to go as part of a tour for access - a full-day. The cheapest price-performance tour is offered by the Barossa Wine Tour company. You can do a full-day tour from $119 AUD. https://barossawinetour.com.au/

Groupon also offers Adelaide wine tour deals worth checking out" https://www.groupon.com.au/browse/adelaide

# Visit the University

The building is stunning. Use your free city bike to get there. Adelaide University boasts four Nobel Peace Prize winners including Sir Howard Walter Florey for the discovery of penicillin. Enjoy the University's stunning grounds. Free guided tours are also run at the site each Sunday at 12.30 pm and on Wednesdays at 11 am. The tours generally take around 45 minutes focussing on the history and the religious significance as well as the beautiful art works

# Cycle to Waterfall Gully

Waterfall Gully has 7 waterfalls, its a beautiful park where you can hike from one waterfall to another. From here you could also hike up to Mount Lofty for some amazing views over the Adelaide. Just put the name into google maps and cycle there. It is a breathtakingly beautiful walk and waterfall.

Note you can't swim there, you will see many "no swimming" signs.

# Visit the Adelaide Oval

Check out some games of AFL or cricket, or just wander by and hear the crowd roar on Friday nights. Cheap tickets can be found here https://www.capitalcitytickets.com/Schedule/Adelaide-Oval-Tickets. Tours of the Oval cost $25.

# Take a free tour of St Peter's Cathedral

St Peters Cathedral was built from 1869 but took many years to complete as funding run out. You can enjoy a free tour of the magnificent gothic architecture every Wednesday at 11:00am.

In the 20th century  Adelaide was knowns the "City of Churches" due to its diversity of faiths.

# Explore 29 parks

Adelaide is home to 29 parks. The locals are kind and friendly and the parks are great meeting places. Adelaide Parklands is great and you'll find the Park Lands are home to many public events, including major events such as WOMADelaide and the Adelaide Fringe Festival.

# Henley Beach

Go at Sunset for spectacular views - cycle or take bus H30, from Stop T2 or U2 Southside. The bus leaves every half hour and takes 35 minutes.

If you love beaches, an hour's drive from Adelaide is another worldly place called Fleurieu Peninsula. It was named after French man Nicolas Baudin in 1802. Here you can find over 30 different whale species as well as beaches, snorkelling, sailing and swimming. You can take the 1251 bus there for under $20.

# Explore Adelaide Central Market

Watch cheese being made and feast on chocolate samples at Adelaide's 143 year old market. The market officially opened on the 22nd January 1870. Shops have replaced the 100's of produce carts but there remains a commitment to gourmet quality. Today Little Khmer Kitchen serves up some of the most original and affordable food in the market.

Afterwards visit Oxfam Books on Hutt Street for some cheap awesome reads for those long bus rides or to find a $1 first-edition book to sell for $500 on eBay.

# Visit Glenelg Beach

It is a beautiful beach town with a main Street to walk with shops and good eateries. You can cycle there with a free bike or take the red line tram.

### Surfing
The beaches in Adelaide don't have surf the upside is that they are a lot less crowded and just as beautiful. While Glenelg is the tourist hotspot, you can head over to Brighton, Henly or Semaphore beaches for a more sedate experience.

# Explore Hahndorf

About 45 minutes up the freeway is a beautiful little German town you will absolutely love. Hahndorf has great shops and atmosphere. Go in fall for the most amazing colours. Take the 864 bus towards Mt Barker.

# The Murray River

Australia's longest river and the third longest river in the world runs through Adelaide.

Take a picnic to Rymill Park and sit by the Murray River or go to Murray Bridge.

Colonel Willian Light's statue on Montefiore Hill is another great picnic spot to relax and marvel at the sights.

## INSIDER INSIGHT

Wild dolphins live in Port River. They are Indo-Pacific bottlenose dolphins. They are wild and free but have chosen to call the Port River heir home.

# Enjoy free workouts

The Goodlife Adelaide City gym offers a FREE 5 Day Pass . They are offering you the pass for free to convert you into a paying member. Don't feel bad, think of all the money you've paid gyms and never used their services. You can also leave them a review online if you feel bad for using their facilities for free.

# Get Cheap cinema tickets

**Mercury Cinema:** is a little different to most.
Being a cinema club, it doesn't offer single tickets; you
need to buy a membership (for four films, ten films or a year
of films). But these are very good value, as you end up paying between $2.50 to $10.00 per screening. The cinema
shows new releases alongside a retrospective program,
however its new releases are generally ones from film festivals or those that aren't getting screened elsewhere.

# Visit Adelaide's Rooftop bars

If you love rooftop bars go to 2KW, The Majestic Hotel or Florence Rooftop Bar. If you're not overly concerned about the view just check out the laneways (off Rundle St or Hindley St) to find cute little bars and great restaurants, there are dozens.

# Watch Free comedy

The Rhino room offers a double free pass ($30) if you enter your details to become an Adelaide Comedy Member. Sign-up here: https://www.rhinoroom.com.au/

# Go thrift shopping (opshopping)

Salvos Stores North Adelaide offers great insight into Adelaide thrifting. Other op shops with huge ranges and very low prices and lots of designer gems include SWOP Clothing Exchange, Goodies Op Shop, Stop By Op Shop and the Australian Red Cross's 'Two 8 Four'.

# Go Book Shopping

Oxfam Books offers a huge range of paperback books for $1!

**Address:** 81-89 Hutt Street

# Score some free stuff

It's not news that the pandemic disrupted supply chains and contributed to major delays in shipping causing prices to increase. Researchers at  at the University of Pennsylvania's Wharton School found that the average American family had to spend roughly $3,500 more in 2021 than in 2020 for the same goods and services due to inflation. One great way to save money in Adelaide is to peruse local Freecycle, Trashnothing and Free in Adelaide Facebook sites. If you find you need to buy something, whether that be a charger or torch in Adelaide check these sites before. You can often find incredible freebies here that will cost you only the time to pick them up. Here is a list of the best free stuff websites in Adelaide:

https://trashnothing.com/beta/adelaide-au-freecycle

https://au.ziilch.com/Adelaide

https://www.gumtree.com.au/s-adelaide/free+stuff/k0l3006878

# Food and drinks hacks

### Bottomless coffee at Hungry Jacks

Go to any Hungry Jacks around the city for unlimited coffee refills and free wifi.

### Best Bang for your buck all-you-can-eat

**Fresh Choice Restaurant** has an all-you-can-eat buffet during the week. The food is great quality and highly nutritious. The buffet costs $20.

Address: 373 Diagonal Rd.

### BYO Alcohol Restaurants
Alcohol in Australia is highly taxed. Look for a restaurant that allows BYO and get a good local bottle from a store. Some great restaurants that offer BYO are:
1. East Taste Cafe
2. Amalfi Pizzeria
3. Parwana
4. 4. New Local Eatery
5. 5. Little NNQ

### If you're in Adelaide on your birthday

You can present your ID to receive a number food of freebies:

Boost – Get a free drink.
Muffin Break – A free muffin to celebrate your big day.
Nandos – You'll get a whole meal on your birthday!
Oporto – Enjoy a meal on them!
Baskin Robbins – One free scoop!
Subway – Free lunch on your birthday.

# Not super cheap but loved

*Port Hughes*

## Visit Port Hughes

Just west of Adelaide, in South Australia's Yorke Peninsula is stunning Port Huges. You can take a bus from the central train station to Moonta Cnr Henry & Milne and a taxi from there. Round-trip is $60.

# Swim with sea lions

You can do this for free at Port Lincoln. You can take a cheap flight there with Jetstar circa $65 single.

# Visit Kangaroo Island

SeaLink operates the ferry service to Kangaroo Island. Each crossing takes **approximately 45 minutes** and departs from Cape Jervis which is a 1.5 hour drive south of Adelaide. It costs 27.50 return. the island is definitely worth the trip but pack snacks. Sealink also operate the bus from Adelaide Central Bus Station to Cape Jervis which costs $17 each way. DO NOT BUY A COMBO TICKET - it works out cheaper as singles and they time the ferries for the bus arrivals.

# Walk the Heysen Trail

This impressive 1,200km walking route. Bus Premier Stateliner is going there for $60 return.

# Explore the outback

Go north up to the Flinders Ranges to experience the outback. It's a 6 hour drive. Prices as low as $60 for the day as a group of 10. Hostels are the best place to book a Flinders Ranges Tour.

# Need to Know

**Currency**: Australian Dollar

**Language**: English / Aussie Slang

**Money**: Widely available ATMs.

**Visas**: http://www.doyouneedvisa.com/

**Mobile Data:**
Many telecoms providers will allow you to roam free in Australia. Check your plan, if not pick up a Telstra prepaid SIM.

**Time**: GMT + 9.5

**When to Go**
High Season: March to May
Shoulder: September to November
Low Season: December to March.
**Important Numbers**
000 Ambulance
000 Police

# Cheap Eats

**Fill your stomach without emptying your wallet by trying these local restaurants with mains under $10 AUD.**

Download the offline map on google maps, (instructions 1. go to app 2. select offline apps in the left sidebar 3. go to the area you want to download 4. click download) then simply type the restaurant names in to navigate, star them so you can see where the cheap eats are when you're out and about to avoid wasting your money at hyped tourist joints.

### The Flying Fig Deli
Bagels (starting at AUD$6.50) and eggs on organic sourdough rye with beetroot remoulade (AUD$9.90).

Address: 161 Jeffcott Street

### Burger Theory
Burger (AUD$10) comes with lettuce, tomato and American cheese in a brioche bun. The Number 2 (AUD$12) features a blue cheese sauce, onion confit and bacon.

Address: 8-10 Union Street.

### Sit Lo
Delve into a cone of crispy lotus root chips for AUD$4.50.

Address: 30 Bank Street

## Lucia's

Poached eggs, tomatoes and mushrooms on artisan bread (AUD$13.50) will fill you up; the spaghetti carbonara (AUD$13.50), and the spaghetti vongole (AUD$15) are also particularly good.

Address: Stall 1, Adelaide Central Market, Grote Street.

## Kutchi Deli Parwana

Wrap your lips around fried dumplings stuffed with leek and topped with lamb mince and split pea sauce (AUD$13). Nibble on chicken pieces marinated in yoghurt and Afghan spices (AUD$15).

Address: 7 Ebenezer Place

## Chinatown Café

Great cheap Chinese food. The Hainanese Chicken with Laksa broth and Asian Greens are incredible and you can sit outside.

Address: 38-41 Moonta Street, Chinatown

## Star of Siam

Probably the best Thai restaurant in town. We recommend trying the the 'sea star' dumplings.

Address: 67 Gouger Street

## Bodri's Hungarian Artisan Bakery & Cafe

Awesome, cheap baked goods in the central market. Try aBur Kifli. A handmade puff pastry filled with the famous Hungarian sweet chestnut puree (gesztenye püré)

**Adelaide City Snack Bar**
Big servings of delicious Vietnamese food for
a cheap price.
Address: 181 Angas Street

**Kutchi Deli Parwana**
Afghani street food dished up in a rustic space with
colourful tiles & traditional decor.

**Warong**
Fast, cheap Halal Asian food served in Rundle Place
Mall. Try the chicken Laksa for $10.

Address: Lower Ground, 77-91 Rundle Mall

**Vietnamese Laundry street food & bar**
Small place making great and cheap food.

Address: 152 Sturt Street

**Bakmi Lim Noodle Project**
Simply delicious cheap and cheerful noodles.

**Pastagogo**
This chain has six outlets across Adleaide and offers amazing pasta fast and cheap.

# Getting out cheaply

At the time of writing Jetstar are offering the cheapest flights onwards. Take advantage of discounts and specials. Sign up for e-newsletters from local carriers including Jetstar to learn about special fares. Be careful with cheap airlines, most will allow hand-luggage only, and some charge for anything that is not a backpack. Check their websites before booking if you need to take luggage.

**Cheapest Bus Out**
Firefly Express is the cheapest bus provider for onward destinations from Adelaide. But it actually works out cheap to fly due to the vast distances you will have to cover.

## Airport Lounges

You don't need to be flying business or first class to enjoy an airport lounge. Here are three methods you can use to access lounges at Adelaide airport:

- Get or use a credit card that gives free lounge access. NerdWallet has a good write-up about cards that offer free lounge access. www.nerdwallet.com/best/credit-cards/airport-lounge-access

- Buy onetime access. They start at $23 and often include free showers and free drinks and food.

- Find free access with the LoungeBuddy app. You pay an annual fee of $25 to use the app.

# Print or screenshot for easy reference

|  | How | Cost normally | Cost when following suggested |
|---|---|---|---|
| **Stay** | airbnb in the city <br><br> $10 | Hotels are upwards of $150 a night. | $10/ night x 5 |
| **Tastiest street foods to try** | Veggie Velo food truck. | $250 eating out. You don't have to spend a lot to | $6 - $10 - two meals out a day. Total cost $60 |
| **Get around** | free bike, free buses | $50 in Ubers | $0 |
| **See** | Beaches, wine valley trips | $300 | $70 half day tour of the vineyards |
| **Get out** | Jetstar to Melbourne $25 | $75 | $25 |
| **Total** |  | $1425 saving $1,220 | $500 |

72

# RECAP: How to have a $3,000 trip to Adelaide on a $500 budget

### Find last-minute Five star hotels

Check on the same day of your stay for cheap five star hotel deals. Go to booking.com enter Adelaide, tonight, only one night and 5 stars. In business cities, such as Adelaide this can be very effective in the low season on the weekends when hotels empty of their business travellers. Potential saving $800.

### Use camper-van relocation to travel to or from Adelaide

Relocating a camper-van can save you a small fortune on trips to Melbourne, Sydney and beyond. Potential saving: $400.

### Restaurant deals

Nearly every restaurant in Adelaide offers a midday menu for lunch at around $7 and happy hour deals from 5pm. If you're on a budget, but like eating out, consider doing your dining in the daytime. And stick to food trucks and happy hours at night. Potential saving $200.

### Stock up on discount produce

NQR and Aldi offer great discounts on fresh produce. If you have somewhere to cook you can find discounted meats and deli goods at Coles and Woolworths.

## Go to museums/ attractions for free
The average traveller spends $80 on attractions in Adelaide but theres no need. The free museums and tours are equally great. Potential saving $80.

## Book a cheaper wine tour
Wine tours of Adelaide's hills and Barossa Valley are big business and average around $300. Check Groupon for last-minute deals and save upwards of $200. If there are no deals BarossaValley.com is the best provider.

## Drink outdoors with friends
Adelaide is super green and the best way to experience the city is to buy a bottle of wine from a supermarket and enjoy somewhere green, or on the beach. A wine costs around $8 in a bar. Potential savings on drinks $50 assuming you have a couple a day - hey you're on vacation!

## Book ahead
Book buses and onward flights six weeks in advance for the cheapest prices.
Potential savings: $150

# Money Mistakes in Adelaide

| Cost | Impact | Solution | Note |
|---|---|---|---|
| Using your home currency | Some credit cards charge for every transaction in another currency. Check carefully before you use it | Use a prepaid currency card like Wise Multi-Currency Debit Card to pay seamlessly in Australian Dollars. | Skip transaction fees! |
| Buying bottled water | At $3 a bottle, this is a cost that can mount up quickly | Refill from the tap. If you're going into more remote areas bring a water bottle like Water-to-go. | |
| Eating like a tourist | Eating at tourist traps can triple your bill. Prices can triple for the same meal. | Favourite cheap eats on google maps so you're never far from one. | |
| Not agreeing a price of everything in advance | Taxi's and other unpriced services allow people to con you. | Agree the price beforehand to avoid unwanted bills. | |
| Not getting your Tax refund | Keep your receipts. You can claim a refund of the goods and services tax (GST) and wine equalisation tax (WET) that you pay on goods you buy in Australia | To claim go to the airport at least 35 minutes to show your passport, boarding pass and original invoices (if you are leaving by sea, reach the port 1-4 hours earlier) Here is how to claim: https://www.abf.gov.au/entering-and-leaving-australia/tourist-refund-scheme | Remember Airport souvenirs are usually way pricier than they'd be in-destination, so grab your souvenirs before heading for the plane |

# The secret to saving HUGE amounts of money when travelling to Adelaide is...

Your mindset. Money is an emotional topic, if you associate words like cheapskate, Miser (and its £9.50 to go into Charles Dickens Adelaide house, oh the Irony) with being thrifty when traveling you are likely to say 'F-it' and spend your money needlessly because you associate pain with saving money. You pay now for an immediate reward. Our brains are prehistoric; they focus on surviving day to day. Travel companies and hotels know this and put trillions into making you believe you will be happier when you spend on their products or services. Our poor brains are up against outdated programming and an onslaught of advertisements bombarding us with the message: spending money on travel equals PLEASURE. To correct this carefully lodged propaganda in your frontal cortex, you need to imagine your future self.

Saving money does not make you a cheapskate. It makes you smart. How do people get rich? They invest their money. They don't go out and earn it; they let their money earn more money. So every time you want to spend money, imagine this: while you travel, your money is working for you, not you for money. While you sleep, the money, you've invested is going up and up. That's a pleasure a pricey entrance fee can't give you. Thinking about putting your money to work for you tricks your brain into believing you are not withholding pleasure from yourself, you are saving your money to invest so you can go to even more amazing places. You are thus turning thrifty travel into a pleasure fueled sport.

When you've got money invested - If you want to splash your cash on a first-class airplane seat - you can. I can't tell you how to invest your money, only that you should. Saving $20 on taxis doesn't seem like much, but over time you could save upwards of $15,000 a year, which is a deposit for a house which you can rent on Airbnb to finance more travel. Your brain making money looks like your brain on cocaine, so tell yourself saving money is making money.

Scientists have proved that imagining your future self is the easiest way to associate pleasure with saving money. You can download FaceApp — which will give you a picture of what you will look like older and grayer, or you can take a deep breath just before spending money and ask yourself if you will regret the purchase later.

The easiest ways to waste money traveling are:
Getting a taxi. The solution to this is to always download the google map before you go. Many taxi drivers will drive you around for 15 minutes when the place you were trying to get to is a 5-minute walk… remember while not getting an overpriced taxi to tell yourself, 'I am saving money to free myself for more travel.'
Spending money on overpriced food when hungry. The solution: carry snacks. A banana and an apple will cost you, in most places, less than a dollar.

Spending on entrance fees to top-rated attractions. If you really want to do it, spend the money happily. If you're conflicted, sleep on it. I don't regret spending $200 on a sky dive over the Great Barrier Reef; I regret going to the top of the shard on a cloudy day in London for $60. Only you can know, but make sure it's your decision and not the marketing directors at said top-rated attraction.

Telling yourself 'you only have the chance to see/eat/experience it now'. While this might be true, make sure YOU WANT to spend the money. Money spent is money you can't invest, and often you can have the same experience for much less.

You can experience luxurious travel on a small budget, which will trick your brain into thinking you're already a high-roller, which will mean you'll be more likely to act like one and invest your money. Stay in five-star hotels for $5 by booking on the day of your stay on booking.com to enjoy last-minute deals. You can go to fancy restaurants using daily deal sites. Ask your airline about last-minute upgrades to first-class or business. I paid $100 extra on a $179 ticket to Cuba from Germany to be bumped to Business Class. When you ask, it will surprise you what you can get both at hotels and airlines.

Travel, as the saying goes, is the only thing you spend money on that makes you richer. You can easily waste money, making it difficult to enjoy that metaphysical wealth. The biggest money saving secret is to turn bargain hunting into a pleasurable activity, not an annoyance. Budgeting consciously can be fun, don't feel disappointed because you don't spend the $60 to go into an attraction. Feel good because soon that $60 will soon earn money for you. Meaning, you'll have the time and money to enjoy more metaphysical wealth while your bank balance increases.

So there it is. You can save a small fortune by being strategic with your trip planning. We've arranged everything in the guide to offer the best bang for your buck. Which means we took the view that if it's not an excellent investment for your money, we wouldn't include it. Why would a guide called 'Super Cheap' include lots of overpriced attractions? That said, if you think we've missed something or have unanswered questions, ping me an email: philgtang@gmail.com I'm on central Europe time and usually reply within 8 hours of getting your mail. We like to think of our guide books as evolving organisms helping our readers travel better cheaper. We use reader questions via email to update this book year round so you'll be helping other readers and yourself.

**Don't put your dreams off!**

Time is a currency you never get back and travel is its greatest return on investment. Plus, now you know you can visit Adelaide for a fraction of the price most would have you believe.

# Thank you for reading

Dear **Lovely Reader**,

**If you have found this book useful, please consider writing a quick review on Amazon.**

One person from every 1000 readers leaves a review on Amazon. It would mean more than you could ever know if you were one of our 1 in 1000 people to take the time to write a brief review.

Thank you so much for reading again and for spending your time and investing your trips future in Super Cheap Insider Guides. One last note, please don't listen to anyone who says 'Oh no, you can't visit Adelaide on a budget'. Unlike you, they didn't have this book. You can do ANYWHERE on a budget with the right insider advice and planning. Sure, learning to travel to Adelaide on a budget that doesn't compromise on anything or drastically compromise on safety or comfort levels is a skill, but this guide has done the detective work for you. Now it is time for you to put the advice into action.

Phil and the Super Cheap Insider Guides Team

P.S If you need any more super cheap tips we'd love to hear from you e-mail me at philgtang@gmail.com, we have a lot of contacts in every region, so if there's a specific bargain you're hunting we can help you find it.

# DISCOVER YOUR NEXT VACATION

☑ **LUXURY ON A BUDGET APPROACH**
☑ **CHOOSE FROM 107 DESTINATIONS**
☑ **EACH BOOK PACKED WITH REAL-TIME LOCAL TIPS**

All are available in Paperback and e-book on Amazon:

https://www.amazon.com/dp/B09C2DHQG5

Several are available as audiobooks. You can watch excerpts of ALL for FREE on YouTube: https://youtube.com/channel/UCxo9YV8-M9P1cFosU-Gjnqg

Super Cheap ALASKA 2023

Super Cheap AMSTERDAM 2023

Super Cheap ANTIGUA 2023

Super Cheap ANTARCTICA 2023

Super Cheap AUSTIN 2023

Super Cheap BANGKOK 2023

Super Cheap BARBADOS 2023

Super Cheap BARCELONA 2023

Super Cheap BATH 2023

Super Cheap BELFAST 2023

Super Cheap BERMUDA 2023

Super Cheap BERLIN 2023

Super Cheap BIRMINGHAM 2023

Super Cheap BORA BORA 2023

Super Cheap BORDEAUX 2023

Super Cheap BRUGES 2023

Super Cheap BUDAPEST 2023

Super Cheap Bahamas 2023

Super Cheap Great Barrier Reef 2023

Super Cheap CABO 2023

Super Cheap CALGARY 2023

Super Cheap CAMBRIDGE 2023

Super Cheap CANCUN 2023

Super Cheap CAPPADOCIA 2023

Super Cheap CAPRI 2023

Super Cheap CARCASSONNE 2023

Super Cheap CHAMPAGNE REGION 2023

Super Cheap CHIANG MAI 2023

Super Cheap CHICAGO 2023

Super Cheap COPENHAGEN 2023

Super Cheap DOHA 2023

Super Cheap DOMINICAN REPUBLIC 2023

Super Cheap DUBAI 2023

Super Cheap DUBLIN 2023

Super Cheap EDINBURGH 2023

Super Cheap FLORENCE 2023

Super Cheap GALAPAGOS ISLANDS 2023

Super Cheap GALWAY 2023

Super Cheap HAVANA 2023

Super Cheap HELSINKI 2023

Super Cheap HONG KONG 2023

Super Cheap HONOLULU 2023

Super Cheap INNSBRUCK 2023

Super Cheap ISTANBUL 2023

Super Cheap KUALA LUMPUR 2023

Super Cheap LA 2023

Super Cheap LAPLAND 2023

Super Cheap LAS VEGAS 2023

Super Cheap LIMA 2023

Super Cheap LISBON 2023

Super Cheap LIVERPOOL 2023

Super Cheap LONDON 2023

Super Cheap MACHU PICHU 2023

Super Cheap MALAGA 2023

Super Cheap MALDIVES 2023

Super Cheap Machu Pichu 2023

Super Cheap MELBOURNE 2023

Super Cheap MIAMI 2023

Super Cheap MONACO 2023

Super Cheap Milan 2023

Super Cheap Munich 2023

Super Cheap NASHVILLE 2023

Super Cheap NEW ORLEANS 2023

Super Cheap NEW YORK 2023

Super Cheap NORWAY 2023

Super Cheap PARIS 2023

Super Cheap PRAGUE 2023

Super Cheap SAN FRANCISCO 2023

Super Cheap Santorini 2023

Super Cheap SEYCHELLES 2023

Super Cheap SINGAPORE 2023

Super Cheap SYDNEY 2023

Super Cheap ST LUCIA 2023

Super Cheap TORONTO 2023

Super Cheap TURKS AND CAICOS 2023

Super Cheap TURIN 2023

Super Cheap VENICE 2023

Super Cheap VIENNA 2023

Super Cheap WASHINGTON 2023

Super Cheap YORK 2023

Super Cheap YOSEMITE 2023

Super Cheap ZURICH 2023

Super Cheap ZANZIBAR 2023

# Bonus Travel Hacks

I've included these bonus travel hacks to help you plan and enjoy your trip to Adelaide cheaply, joyfully, and smoothly. Perhaps they will even inspire you to start or renew a passion for long-term travel.

When I tell people I write a travel guide series focused on luxurious budget travel, they wrongly assume that's impossible and often say 'Hitchhiking and couch-surfing?'. Others with more vivid imaginations ask me if I recommend hooking up with older men or women... they are surprised when I tell them that not one of the 107 Super Cheap Guides endorses such practises because they maximise discomfort. They look at me dumbfounded and ask 'How on earth do you travel luxuriously on a budget then?'

Travelling cheaply in a way that doesn't compromise enjoyment, comfort or safety is a skill I have honed over 20 years of travelling. My foremost learning was that locals always know the tricks and tips to enjoy the same or a better tourist experience for a 10th of the cost, and that's why I teamed up with locals in each locale to distil the tips that will save you a fortune without compromising on enjoyment or comfort.

Enjoyable budget travel is about balancing and prioritising what is important to you.

When I tell people about my method I often receive long defensive monologues about why they spend so much on travel, or why they can't or don't travel. That's why we will first discuss how you can find the freedom to travel.

**How to find the freedom to travel**

'Freedom is one of those words that can mean different things to different people. It's important to be clear on what it looks like to you in your life, and all the stories and beliefs that prevent you from having it. For me, freedom means always having at choice in my life. I don't do anything that I don't want to do.' —LEO BABAUTA

We've spoken a lot about how to save money travelling to Adelaide, but how do you find the freedom if you have:

1.  Pets

2.  Kids

3.  A spouse who doesn't want you to travel

4.  A job that keeps you at home?

Like everything, there's a solution to every problem. In this chapter, I want to you to think about whether your excuses can be overcome using the following solutions, because as Randy Komisar said: "And then there is the most dangerous risk of all – the risk of spending your life not doing what you want on the bet you can buy yourself the freedom to do it later."

**Pets**

I have a dog, an extremely loving German Shepherd. And when I travel overland from Austria, she comes with me and my wife. If we are heading on a longer trip we either leave her with friends or family or we get someone to house sit for us. housesitters.com offers people who are vetted and reviewed and in exchange for free accommodation will care for your pets. Just be aware it often works out financially better to rent your space on Airbnb and pay someone to look after your pets. Make sure you visit their facilities before you entrust your pet to anyone and of course, always read the reviews.

I know a lot of people miss their pets travelling which is why we endeavour to take our dog with us. Exploring with her has formed some of our most precious memories. If you're flying with your pet always look up the rules and make sure you comply. If you're going to the UK for example, they quarantine dogs who come in by air. So we only take our dog by car. Coming into the UK by car, dogs must need to be chipped, have a note from a vet saying they are clear of Rabies and tapeworms, have a pet passport and be on a course of medication for tapeworms 2 days before they enter. The UK is the strictest country I've encountered when it comes to travelling with pets so I use this as barometer. My point is, do your homework if you're bringing your furry friend, both about entry conditions and the local environment for your pet. For instance, in India, many domesticated dogs are attacked by street dogs. Educate yourself on your options and limitations but don't think because you have pets that travel is out of the question.

## Kids

I have two daughters, 2 years and 5 months at the time of writing. If your destination allows, the easiest way to travel with kids is in an RV. You don't have to worry about checking vast amounts of baggage or travelling with a stroller. You have unlimited freedom and can camp for free in many places. You can normally take the RV on a slow ship cheaper than the price of a plane ticket for 3 people.

Travelling is great for kids. A study by Cornell University found that we get more happiness from anticipating a travel experience compared to anticipating buying a new possession, so in that way, money can buy you happiness. If you invest in an RV, you can also turn it into a profit centre by renting it out on platforms like www.outdoorsy.com.

You don't necessarily have to fly to travel with kids, train, bus, cruise and RV's are better options. Kids become more adaptable and flexible when the world is their classroom. This is true at any age. But when kids immerse themselves in unknown places and engage with local cultures; this open-mindedness helps them in all aspects of their lives. For school-age children, you are limited to holiday dates, but with 12 weeks off a year, you can still find adventure together.

## A spouse who doesn't want you to travel

A loving partner should always want what's best for you. Scientifically, travelling is proven to reduce stress. A study in 2000 study found that men and women who do not take a trip for several years are 30 percent more likely to have a heart attack. It makes sense because when you travel you are more active; travellers often walk ten miles a day, sight-seeing and soaking up new sights and smells.

Travelling also strengthens the 'openness' aspect of your personality and makes you less emotionally reactive to day-to-day changes, improving emotional stability. Sure, losing your baggage or almost missing a connecting flight can be panic-inducing, but overall, the data supports travelling is beneficial for you. Tell your partner about these studies. If they don't want a healthier, happier, more emotionally stable you, then it may be time to consider why you're investing your time with this person.

Another common issue is mismatched travel budgets. If you and your partner travel together and they force you to overspend with the 'we're on holiday/vacation!' appendage, here's a tip from one of our writers, Kim:

'My husband and I always had 'discussions' about money during our trips. I love bargains and he is the traveller who's totally cool to be ripped off because he normally travels for business and has become used to spending corporate money. The compromise we reached is that he reads a shoestring or super cheap guide before the trip. Then when he wants to waste money, I say yes, but only in exchange for doing one budget item from the guide. It has worked wonders, lessened our 'discussions' and he now actually chooses cheaper destinations as he sees budgeting as a game.'

## A job that keeps you at home

Our lives can feel constantly busy. Sometimes we may feel we are sinking beneath our workload. If you're close to or suffering a burnout, the stress relief that comes from novelty and change in the form of new people, sights and experiences is the best remedy you could give to yourself.

If you're in a job that is hurting your health or well-being, it's time to reconsider why. Often you believe the work to be deeply rewarding, but if that reward leaves you ill, uninspired, and fatigued, you can't help anyone. I learnt this the hard way when I worked for a charity whose mission I deeply resonated with. After 3 years of 70 hour work weeks, I'd lost hair, teeth, direction and, if I'm honest, faith in humanity. It took me 3 years to come back to the light and see that I chose a very stressful job that my body told me repeatedly it could not handle. Travel was a big part of forgiving myself. It helped me put old stories that held me back and probably sent me into this quagmire of self-abuse via work into perspective.

Sometimes we keep letting ourselves make excuses about why we're not travelling, because we fear the unknown. In such cases, one of three things happens that forces a person from their nest:

- A traumatic event

- Completing a major milestone

- A sudden realisation or epiphany

Do yourself a favour, don't wait for any of those. Decide you want to travel, and book a flight. Our next section takes you through how to book the cheapest possible flight.

# MORE TIPS TO FIND CHEAP FLIGHTS

"The use of travelling is to regulate imagination by reality, a nd instead of thinking how things may be, to see them as t hey are." Samuel Jackson

If you're working full-time, you can save yourself a lot of money by requesting your time off from work starting in the middle of the week. Tuesdays and Wednesdays are the cheapest days to fly. You can save thousands just by adjusting your time off.

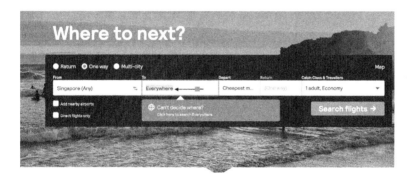

The simplest secret to booking cheap flights is open parameters. Let's say you want to fly from Chicago to Paris. You enter the USA in from and select France under to. You may find flights from New York City to Paris for $70. Then you just need to find a cheap flight to NYC. Make sure you calculate full costs, including if you need airport accommodation and of course getting to and from airports, **but in nearly every instance open parameters will save you at least half the cost of the flight.**

If you're not sure about where you want to go, use open parameters to show you the cheapest destinations from your city. Start with skyscanner.net they include the low-cost airlines that others like Kayak leave out. Google Flights can also show you cheap destinations. To see these leave the WHERE TO section blank.

Open parameters can also show you the cheapest dates to fly. If you're flexible, you can save up to 80% of the flight cost. Always check the weather at your destination before you book. Sometimes a $400 flight will be $20, because it's monsoon season. But hey, if you like the rain, why not?

## ALWAYS USE A PRIVATE BROWSER TO BOOK FLIGHTS

Skyscanner and other sites track your IP address and put prices up and down based on what they determine your strength of conviction to buy. e.g. if you've booked one-way and are looking for the return, these sites will jack the prices up by in most cases 50%. Incognito browsing pays.

### Use a VPN such as Hola to book your flight from your destination

Install Hola, change your destination to the country you are flying to. The location from which a ticket is booked can affect the price significantly as algorithms consider local buying power.

### Choose the right time to buy your ticket.

Choose the right time to buy your ticket, as purchasing tickets on a Sunday has been proven to be cheaper. If you can only book during the week, try to do it on a Tuesday.

### Mistake fares

Email alerts from individual carriers are where you can find the best 'mistake fares". This is where a computer error has resulted in an airline offering the wrong fare. In my experience, it's best to sign up to individual carriers email lists, but if you ARE lazy Secret Flying puts together a daily roster of mistake fares. Visit https://www.secretflying.com/errorfare/ to see if there're any errors that can benefit you.

### Fly late for cheaper prices

Red-eye flights, the ones that leave later in the day, are typically cheaper and less crowded, so aim to book that flight if possible. You will also get through the airport much quicker at the end of the day. Just make sure there's ground transport available for when you land. You don't want to save $50 on the airfare and spend it on a taxi to your accommodation.

### Use this APP for same day flights

If your plans are flexible, use 'Get The Flight Out' (http://www.gtfoflights.com/) a fare tracker Hopper that shows you same-day deeply discounted flights. This is best for long-haul flights with major carriers. You can often find a British Airways round-trip from JFK Airport to Heathrow for $300. If you booked this in advance, you'd pay at least double.

### Take an empty water bottle with you

Airport prices on food and drinks are sky high. It disgusts me to see some airports charging $10 for a bottle of water. ALWAYS take an empty water bottle with you. It's relatively unknown, but most airports have drinking water fountains past the security check. Just type in your airport name to wateratairports.com to locate the fountain. Then once you've passed security (because they don't allow you to take 100ml or more of liquids) you can freely refill your bottle with water.

### Round-the-World (RTW) Tickets

It is always cheaper to book your flights using a DIY approach. First, you may decide you want to stay longer in one country, and a RTW will charge you a hefty fee for changing your flight. Secondly, it all depends on where and when you travel and as we have discussed, there are many ways to ensure you pay way less than $1,500 for a year of flights. If you're travelling long-haul, the best strategy is to buy a return ticket, say New York, to Bangkok and then take cheap flights or transport around Asia and even to Australia and beyond.

## Cut your costs to and from airports

Don't you hate it when getting to and from the airport is more expensive than your flight! And this is true in so many cities, especially European ones. For some reason, Google often shows the most expensive options. Use Omio to compare the cheapest transport options and save on airport transfer costs.

## Car sharing instead of taxis

Check if Adelaide has car sharing at the airport. Often they'll be tons of cars parked at the airport that are half the price of taking a taxi into the city. In most instances, you register your driving licence on an app and scan the code on the car to get going.

## Checking Bags

Sometimes you need to check bags. If you do, put an AirTag inside. That way, you'll be about to see when you land where your bag is. This saves you the nail biting wait at baggage claim. And if worse comes to worst, and you see your bag is actually in another city, you can calmly stroll over to customer services and show them where your bag is.

## Is it cheaper and more convenient to send your bags ahead?

Before you check your bags, check if it's cheaper to send them ahead of you with sendmybag.com obviously if you're staying in an Airbnb, you'll need to ask the hosts permission or you can time them to arrive the day after you. Hotels are normally very amenable.

# What Credit Card Gives The Best Air Miles?

You can slash the cost of flights just for spending on a piece of plastic.

**LET'S TALK ABOUT DEBT**

Before we go into the best cards for each country, let's first talk about debt. The US system offers the best and biggest rewards. Why? Because they rely on the fact that many people living in the US will not pay their cards in full and the card will earn the bank significant interest payments. Other countries have a very different attitude towards money, debt, and saving than Americans. Thus in Germany and Austria the offerings aren't as favourable as the UK, Spain and Australia, where debt culture is more widely embraced. The takeaway here is this: **Only spend on one of these cards when you have set-up an automatic total monthly balance repayment. Don't let banks profit from your lizard brain!**

**The best air-mile credit cards for those living in the UK**

Amex Preferred Rewards Gold comes out top for those living in the UK for 2023.

Here are the benefits:

- 20,000-point bonus on £3,000 spend in first three months. These can be used towards flights with British Airways, Virgin Atlantic, Emirates and Etihad, and often

other rewards, such as hotel stays and car hire.
- 1 point per £1 spent
- 1 point = 1 airline point
- Two free visits a year to airport lounges
- No fee in year one, then £140/yr

The downside:

- Fail to repay fully and it's 59.9% rep APR interest, incl fee

You'll need to cancel before the £140/yr fee kicks in year two if you want to avoid it.

## The best air-mile credit cards for those living in Canada

Aeroplan is the superior rewards program in Canada. The card has a high earn rate for Aeroplan Points, generating 1.5 points per $1 spent on eligible purchases. Look at the specifics of the eligible purchases https://www.aircanada.com/ca/en/aco/home/aeroplan/earn.html. If you're not spending on these things AMEX's Membership Rewards program offers you the best returns in Canada.

## The best air-mile credit cards for those living in Germany

If you have a German bank account, you can apply for a Lufthansa credit card.

Earn 50,000 award miles if you spend $3,000 in purchases and paying the annual fee, both within the first 90 days.

Earn 2 award miles per $1 spent on ticket purchases directly from Miles & More integrated airline partners.

Earn 1 award mile per $1 spent on all other purchases.

The downsides

the €89 annual fee

Limited to fly with Lufthansa and its partners but you can capitalise on perks like the companion pass and airport lounge vouchers.

You need excellent credit to get this card.

**The best air-mile credit cards for those living in Austria**

"In Austria, Miles & More offers you a special credit card. You get miles for each purchase with the credit card. The Miles & More program calculates miles earned based on the distance flown and booking class. For European flights, the booking class is a flat rate. For intercontinental flights, mileage is calculated by multiplying the booking class by the distance flown." They offer a calculator so you can see how many points you could earn: https://www.miles-and-more.com/at/en/earn/airlines/mileage-calculator.html

**The best air-mile credit cards for those living in Spain:**

"The American Express card is the best known and oldest to earn miles, thanks to its membership Rewards program. When making payments with this card, points are added, which can then be exchanged for miles from airlines such as Iberia, Air Europa, Emirates or Alitalia." More information is available here: https://www.americanexpress.com/es-es/

**The best air-mile credit cards for those living in Australia**

ANZ Rewards Black comes out top for 2023.

180,000 bonus ANZ Reward Points (can get an $800 gift card) and $0 annual fee for the first year with the ANZ Rewards Black
Points Per Spend: 1 Velocity point on purchases of up to

$5,000 per statement period and 0.5 Velocity points there-after.

Annual Fee: $0 in the first year, then $375 after.

Ns no set minimum income required, however, there is a minimum credit limit of $15,000 on this card.

Here are some ways you can hack points onto this card: https://www.pointhacks.com.au/credit-cards/anz-rewards-black-guide/

**The best air-mile credit card solution for those living in the USA with a POOR credit score**

The downside to Airline Mile cards is that they require good or excellent credit scores, meaning 690 or higher.

If you have bad credit and want to use credit card air lines you will need to rebuild your credit poor. The Credit One Bank® Platinum Visa® for Rebuilding Credit is a good credit card for people with bad credit who don't want to place a deposit on a secured card. The Credit One Platinum Visa offers a $300 credit limit, rewards, and the potential for credit-limit increases, which in time will help rebuild your score.

**PLEASE don't sign-up for any of these cards if you can't trust yourself to repay it in full monthly. This will only lead to stress for you.**

# Frequent Flyer Memberships

"Points" and "miles" are often used interchangeably, but they're usually two very different things. Maximise and diversify your rewards by utilising both.

A frequent-flyer program (FFP) is a loyalty program offered by an airline. They are designed to encourage airline customers to fly more to accumulate points (also called miles, kilometres, or segments) which can be redeemed for air travel or other rewards.

You can sign up with any FFP program for free. There are three major airline alliances in the world: Oneworld, SkyTeam and Star Alliance. I am with One World https://www.oneworld.com/members because the points can be accrued and used for most flights.

The best return on your points is to use them for international business or first class flights with lie-flat seats. You would need 3 times more miles compared to an economy flight, but if you paid cash, you'd pay 5 - 10 times more than the cost of the economy flight, so it really pays to use your points only for upgrades. The worst value for your miles is to buy an economy seat or worse, a gift from the airlines gift-shop.

Sign up for a family/household account to pool miles together. If you share a common address, you can claim the miles with most airlines. You can use AwardWallet to keep track of your miles. Remember that they only last for 2 years, so use them before they expire.

# How to get 70% off a Cruise

An average cruise can set you back $4,000. If you dream of cruising the oceans, but find the pricing too high, look at repositioning cruises. You can save as much as 70% by taking a cruise which takes the boat back to its home port.

These one-way itineraries take place during low cruise seasons when ships have to reposition themselves to locations where there's warmer weather.

To find a repositioning cruise, go to vacationstogo.com/repositioning_cruises.cfm. This simple and often overlooked booking trick is great for avoiding long flights with children and can save you so much money!

It's worth noting we don't have any affiliations with any travel service or provider. The links we suggest are chosen based on our experience of finding the best deals.

# Pack like a Pro

"He who would travel happily must travel light." – Antoine de St. Exupery 59.

Travel as lightly as you can. We always need less than we think. You will be very grateful that you have a light pack when changing trains, travelling through the airport, catching a bus, walking to your accommodation, or climbing stairs.

Make a list of what you will wear for 7 days and take only those clothes. You can easily wash your things while you're travelling if you stay in an Airbnb with a washing machine or visit a local laundrette. Roll your clothes for maximum space usage and fewer wrinkles. If you feel really nervous about travelling with such few things, make sure you have a dressier outfit, a little black dress for women is always valuable, a shirt for men. Then pack shorts, a long pair of pants, loose tops and a hoodie to snuggle in. Remind yourself that a lack of clothing options is an opportunity to find bargain new outfits in thrift stores. You can either sell these on eBay after you've worn them or post them home to yourself. You'll feel less stressed, as you don't have to look after or feel weighed down by excess baggage. Here are three things to remember when packing:

- Co-ordinate colours - make sure everything you bring can be worn together.

- Be happy to do laundry - fresh clothes when you're travelling feels very luxurious.

- Take liquid minis no bigger than 60ml. Liquid is heavy, and you simply don't need to carry so much at one time.

- Buy reversible clothes (coats are a great idea), dresses which can be worn multiple different ways.

## Checks to Avoid Fees

### Always have 6 months' validity on your passport

To enter most countries, you need 6 months from the day you land. Factor in different time zones around the world if your passport is on the edge. Airport security will stop you from boarding your flight at the airport if your passport has 5 months and 29 days left.

### Google Your Flight Number before you leave for the airport

Easily find out where your plane is from anywhere. Confirm the status of your flight before you leave for the airport with flightaware.com. This can save you long unnecessary wait times.

### Check-in online

The founder, Ryan O'Leary of budget airline Ryanair famously said: "We think they should pay €60 for [failing to check-in online] being so stupid.". Always check-in online, even for international flights. Cheaper international carriers like Scoot will charge you at the airport to check-in.

### Checking Bags

Never, ever check a bag if you can avoid it. Sometimes you need to check bags. If you do, put an AirTag inside. That way, you'll be about to see when you land where your bag is. This saves you the nail biting wait at baggage claim. And if worse comes to worst, and you see your bag is actually in another city, you can calmly stroll over to customer services and show them where your bag is.

## Is it cheaper and more convenient to send your bags ahead?

Before you check your bags, check if it's cheaper to send them ahead of you with sendmybag.com obviously if you're staying in an Airbnb, you'll need to ask the hosts permission or you can time them to arrive the day after you. Hotels are normally very amenable.

It is always cheaper to put heavier items on a ship, rather than take them on a flight with you. Find the best prices for shipping at https://www.parcelmonkey.com/delivery-services/shipping-heavy-items

## Use a fragile sticker

Put a 'Fragile' sticker on anything you check to ensure that it's handled better as it goes through security. It'll also be one of the first bags released after the flight, getting you out of the airport quicker.

## If you check your bag, photograph it

Take a photo of your bag before you check it. This will speed up the paperwork if it is damaged or lost.

# Relaxing at the Airport

The best way to relax at the airport is in a lounge where they provide free food, drinks, comfortable chairs, luxurious amenities (many have showers) and, if you're lucky, a peaceful ambience. If you're there for a longer time, look for Airport Cubicles, sleep pods which charge by the hour.

You can use your FFP Card (Frequent Flyer Memberships) to get into select lounges for free. Check your eligibility before you pay.

If you're travelling a lot, I'd recommend investing in a Priority Pass for the airport.

It includes 850-plus airport lounges around the world. The cost is $99 for the year and $27 per lounge visit or you can pay $399 for the year all inclusive.

If you need a lounge for a one-off day, you can get a Day Pass. Buy it online for a discount, it always works out cheaper than buying at the airport. Use www.LoungePass.com.

Lounges are also great if you're travelling with kids, as they're normally free for kids and will definitely cost you less than snacks for your little ones. The rule is that kids should be seen and not heard, so consider this before taking an overly excited child who wants to run around, or you might be asked to leave even after you've paid.

# Money: How to make it, spend it and save it while travelling

# How to earn money WHILE travelling

"Twenty years from now you will be more disappointed by the things you didn't do than by the ones you did do. So throw off the bowlines. Sail away from the safe harbour." - H. Jackson Brown

Digital nomads receive a lot of hype. Put simply, they are " professionals who work online and therefore don't need to tie themselves to one particular office, city, or even country."

The first step in becoming a digital nomad, earning money while travelling, is knowing what you can offer. Your market is the entire world. So, what product or service would you like to offer that they would pay for? Take some time to think about this. In German, they say you should do whatever comes easily to your hand. For example, I've always loved finding bargains, it comes easily to me. Yet I studied Law and Finance at University, which definitely did not come easy. It's not a shock that it didn't transpire into a career. And served more as a lesson in not following my ego.

There are thousands of possibilities to generate income while travelling; offering services like tutorial, coaching, writing service, PR, blogging. Most travellers I meet try their hand at blogging and earning from the advertisements. This is great if you have some savings, but if you need to earn straight away to travel, this should be on the back burner, as it takes time to establish. Still, if this comes easily to you, do it!

You want to make good money fast. Ask yourself, what is it you are good at and how can you deliver maximum value to other people? Here are some ideas if you're totally dumfounded:

Teaching English online - you will need a private room for this. Be aware that if you're from the USA and the country you want to work in requires a federal-level background check, it may take months, so apply early. Opportunities are on: t.vipkid.com.cn, abc360.com, italki.com, verbalplanet.com and verbling.com. You can expect to earn $20 an hour.

Work in a hostel. Normally you'll get some cash and free accommodation.

Fruit picking. I picked Bananas in Tully, Australia for $20 an hour. The jobs are menial but can be quite meditative. Look on WWOOF.org for organic farm work. There are also amazing opportunities on worldpacker.com and workaway.com

fiverr.com - offer a small service, like making a video template and changing the content for each buyer.

Do freelance work online: marketing, finance, writing, App creation, graphic designer, UX or UI designer, SEO optimiser / expert. Create a profile on upwork.com - you need to put in a lot of work to make this successful, but if you have a unique skill like coding or marketing, it can be very lucrative.

Make a udemy.com course. Can you offer a course in something people will pay for? e.g. stock trading, knitting or marketing.

Use Skype to deliver all manner of services: language lessons, therapy, coaching etc. Google for what you could offer. Most specialisms have a platform you can use to find clients and they will take a cut of your earnings/ require a fee.

You could work on luxury yachts in the med. It's hard work, but you can save money - DesperateSailors.com

Become an Airbnb experience host - but this requires you to know one place and stay there for a time. And you will need a work visa for that country.

Work on a cruise ship. This isn't a digital nomad job but it will help you travel and save at the same time.

Rent your place out on Airbnb while you travel and get a cleaner to manage it. The easiest solution if you own or have a long-term rent contract.

**Passive Income Ideas that earn $1000+ a month**

- Start a YouTube Channel.

- Start a Membership Website.

- Write a Book.

- Create a Lead Gen Website for Service Businesses.

- Join the Amazon Affiliate Program.

- Market a Niche Affiliate Opportunity.

- Create an Online Course.

- Invest in Real Estate

# How to spend money

Bank ATM fees vary from $2.50 per transaction to as high as $5 or more, depending on the ATM and the country. You can completely skip those fees by paying with card and using a card which can hold multiple currencies.

Budget travel hacking begins with a strategy to spend without fees. Your individual strategy depends on the country you legally reside in as to what cards are available. Happily there are some fin-tech solutions which can save you thousands on those pesky ATM withdrawal fees and are widely available globally. Here are a selection of cards you can pre-charge with currency for Adelaide:

## N26

N26 is a 12-year-old digital bank. I have been using them for over 6 years. The key advantage is fee-free card transactions abroad. They have a very elegant app, where you can check your timeline for all transactions listed in real time or manage your in-app security anywhere. The card you receive is a Mastercard so you can use it everywhere. If you lose the card, you don't have to call anyone, just open the app and swipe 'lock card'. It puts your purchases into a graph automatically so you can see what you spend on. You can open an account from abroad entirely online, all you need is your passport and a camera n26.com

### Revolut

Revolut is a multi-currency account that allows you to hold and exchange 29 currencies and spend fee-free abroad. It's a UK based neobank, but accepts customers from all over the world.

### Wise debit card

If you're going to be in one place for a long time, the Wise debit card is like having your travel money on a card – it lets you spend money at the real exchange rate.

### Monzo

**Monzo** is good if your UK based. They offer a fee-free UK account. Fee-free international money transfers and fee-free spending abroad.

### The downside

The cards above are debit cards, meaning you need to have money in those accounts to spend it. This comes with one big downside: safety. Credit card issuers' have "zero liability" meaning you're not liable for unauthorised charges. All the cards listed above do provide cover for unauthorised charges but times vary greatly in how quickly you'd get your money back if it were stolen.

The best option is to check in your country to see which credit cards are the best for travelling and set up monthly payments to repay the whole amount so you don't pay unnecessary interest. In the USA, Schwab regularly ranks at the top for travel credit cards. Credit cards are always the safer option when abroad simply because you get your money back faster if its stolen and if you're renting cars, most will give you free insurance when you book the car rental using the card, saving you money.

**Always withdraw money; never exchange.**

Money exchanges, whether they be on the streets or in the airports will NEVER give you a good exchange rate. Do not bring bundles of cash. Instead, withdraw local currency from the ATM as needed and try to use only free ATMs. Many in airports charge you a fee to withdraw cash. Look for bigger ATMs attached to banks to avoid this.

**Recap**

- Take cash from local, non-charging ATMs for the best rates.

- Never change at airport exchange desks unless you absolutely have to, then just change just enough to be able get to a bank ATM.

- Bring a spare credit card for emergencies.

- Split cash in various places on your person (pockets, shoes) and in your luggage. It's never sensible to keep your cash or cards all in one place.

- In higher risk areas, use a money belt under your clothes or put $50 in your shoe or bra.

### Revolut

Revolut is a multi-currency account that allows you to hold and exchange 29 currencies and spend fee-free abroad. It's a UK based neobank, but accepts customers from all over the world.

### Wise debit card

If you're going to be in one place for a long time the Wise debit card is like having your travel money on a card – it lets you spend money at the real exchange rate.

### Monzo

**Monzo** is good if your UK based. They offer a fee-free UK account. Fee-free international money transfers and fee-free spending abroad.

### The downside

The cards above are debit cards, meaning you need to have money in those accounts to spend it. This comes with one big downside: safety. Credit card issuers' have "zero liability" meaning you're not liable for unauthorised charges. All of the cards listed above do provide cover for unauthorised charges but times vary greatly in how quickly you'd get your money back if it were stolen.

The best option is to check in your country to see which credit cards are the best for travelling and set up monthly payments to repay the whole amount so you don't pay unnecessary interest. In the USA, Schwab[2] regularly ranks at the top for travel credit cards. Credit cards are always the safer option when abroad simply because you get your

---

[2] Charles Schwab High Yield Checking accounts refund every single ATM fee worldwide, require no minimum balance and have no monthly fee.

money back faster if its stolen and if you're renting cars, most will give you free insurance when you book the car rental using the card, saving you money.

**Always withdraw money; never exchange.**

Money exchanges whether they be on the streets or in the airports will NEVER give you a good exchange rate. Do not bring bundles of cash. Instead withdraw local currency from the ATM as needed and try to use only free ATM's. Many in airports charge you a fee to withdraw cash. Look for bigger ATM's attached to banks to avoid this.

**Recap**

- Take cash from local, non-charging ATMs for the best rates.
- Never change at airport exchange desks unless you absolutely have to, then just change just enough to be able get to a bank ATM.
- Bring a spare credit card for emergencies.
- Split cash in various places on your person (pockets, shoes) and in your luggage. Its never sensible to keep your cash or cards all in one place.
- In higher risk areas, use a money belt under your clothes or put $50 in your shoe or bra.

# How to save money while travelling

Saving money while travelling sounds like an oxymoron, but it can be done with little to no effort. Einstein is credited as saying, "Compound interest is the eighth wonder of the world." If you saved and invested $100 today, in 20 years, it would be $2,000 thanks to the power of compound interest. It makes sense then to save your money, invest and make even more money.

The Acorns app is a simple system for this. It rounds up your credit card purchases and puts the rest into a savings account. So if you pay for a coffee and its $3.01, you'll save 0.99 cents. You won't even notice you're saving by using this app: www.acorns.com

Here are some more generic ways you can always save money while travelling:

**Device Safety**

Having your phone, iPad or laptop stolen is one BIG and annoying way you can lose money travelling. The simple solution is to use apps to track your devices. Some OSes have this feature built-in. Prey will try your smartphones or laptops (preyproject.com).

**Book New Airbnb's**

When you take a risk on a new Airbnb listing, you save money. Just make sure the hosts profile is at least 3 years old and has reviews.

### If you end up in an overcrowded city

The website https://campspace.com/ is like Airbnb for camping in people's garden and is a great way to save money if you end up in a city during a big event.

### Look out for free classes

Lots of hostels offer free classes for guests. If you're planning to stay in a hostel, check out what classes your hostel offers. I have learnt languages, cooking techniques, dance styles, drawing and all manner of things for free by taking advantage of free classes at hostels.

### Get student discounts

If you're studying buy an ISIC card - International Student Identity Card. It is internationally recognised, valid in 133 countries and offers more than 150,000 discounts!

### Get Senior Citizen discounts

Most state run attractions, ie, museums, galleries will offer a discount for people over 65 with ID.

### Instal maps.me

Maps me is extremely good for travelling without data. It's like offline google maps without the huge download size.

### Always buy travel insurance

Don't travel without travel insurance. It is a small cost to pay compared with what could be a huge medical bill.

### Travel Apps That'll Make Budget Travel Easier

Travel apps are useful for booking and managing travel logistics. They have one fatal downside: they can track you in the app and keep prices up. If you face this, access the site from an incognito browser tab.

Here are the best apps and what they can do for you:

- Best For flight Fare-Watching: Hopper.

- Best for booking flights: Skyscanner and Google Flights

- Best for timing airport arrivals: FlightAware - check on delays, cancellations and gate changes.

- Best for overcoming a fear of flying: SkyGuru - turbulence forecasts for the route you're flying.

- Best for sharing your location: TripWhistle - text or send your GPS coordinates or location easily.

- Best for splitting expenses among co-travellers: Splittr, Trip Splitter, Venmo or Splitwise.

# How NOT to be ripped off

"One of the great things about travel is that you find out how many good, kind people there are."
— Edith Wharton

The quote above may seem ill placed in a chapter entitled how not to be ripped off, but I included it to remind you that the vast majority of people do not want to rip you off. In fact, scammers are normally limited to three situations:

1.    Around heavily visited attractions - these places are targeted purposively due to sheer footfall. Many criminals believe ripping people off is simply a numbers game.

2.    In cities or countries with low-salaries or communist ideologies. If they can't make money in the country, they seek to scam foreigners. If you have travelled to India, Morocco or Cuba you will have observed this phenomenon.

3.    When you are stuck and the person helping you know you have limited options.

Scammers know that most people will avoid confrontation. Don't feel bad about utterly ignoring someone and saying no. Here are six strategies to avoid being ripped off:

1.    **Never ever agree to pay as much as you want. Always decide on a price before.**

Whoever you're dealing with is trained to tell you, they are uninterested in money. This is a trap. If you let people do this they will ask for MUCH MORE money at the end, and because you have used there service, you will feel obliged to pay. This is a conman's trick and nothing more.

## 2. Pack light

You can move faster and easier. If you take heavy luggage, you will end up taking taxis which are comparatively very costly over time.

## 3. NEVER use the airport taxi service. Plan to use public transport before you reach the airport.

## 4. Don't buy a sim card from the airport. Buy from the local supermarkets it will cost 50% less.

## 5. Eat at local restaurants serving regional food

Food defines culture. Exploring all delights available to the palate doesn't need to cost enormous sums.

6. **Ask the locals what something should cost,** and try not to pay over that.

7. **If you find yourself with limited options.** e.g. your taxi dumps you on the side of the road because you refuse to pay more (common in India and parts of South America) don't act desperate and negotiate as if you have other options or you will be extorted.

## 8. Don't blindly rely on social media[3]

Let's say you post in a Facebook group that you want tips for travelling to The Maldives. A lot of the comments you will receive come from guides, hosts and restaurants doing their own promotion. It's estimated that 50% or more of

---

[3] https://arstechnica.com/tech-policy/2019/12/social-media-plat-forms-leave-95-of-reported-fake-accounts-up-study-finds/

Facebook's current monthly active users are fake.  And what's worse, a recent study found Social media platforms leave 95% of reported fake accounts up. These accounts are the digital versions of the men who hang around the Grand Palace in Bangkok telling tourists its closed, to divert you to shops where they will receive a commission for bringing you.

It can also be the case that genuine comments come from people who have totally different interests, beliefs and yes, budgets to yours. Make your experience your own and don't believe every comment you read.

Bottom line: use caution when accepting recommendations on social media and always fact-check with your own research.

**Small tweaks on the road add up to big differences in your bank balance**

**Take advantage of other hotel amenities**

If you fancy a swim but you're nowhere near the ocean, try the nearest hotel with a pool. As long as you buy a drink, the hotel staff will probably grant you access.

**Fill up your mini bar for free.**

Fill up your mini bar for free by storing things from the breakfast bar or grocery shop in your mini bar to give you a greater selection of drinks and food without the hefty price tag.

**Save yourself some ironing**

Use the steam from the shower to get rid of wrinkles in clothing. If something is creased, leave it trapped with the steam in the bathroom overnight for even better results.

### See somewhere else for free

Opt for long stopovers, allowing you to experience another city without spending much money.

### Wear your heaviest clothes

On the plane to save weight in your pack, allowing you to bring more with you. Big coats can then be used as pillows to make your flight more comfortable.

### Don't get lost while you're away.

Find where you want to go using Google Maps, then type 'OK Maps' into the search bar to store this information for offline viewing.

### Use car renting services

Share Now or Car2Go allow you to hire a car for 2 hours for $25 in a lot of European countries.

### Share Rides

Use sites like blablacar.com to find others who are driving in your direction. It can be 80% cheaper than normal transport. Just check the drivers reviews.

### Use free gym passes

Get a free gym day pass by googling the name of a local gym and free day pass.

### When asked by people providing you a service where you are from..

If there's no price list for the service you are asking for, when asked where you are from, Say you are from a lesser-known poorer country. I normally say Macedonia, and if they don't know where it is, add it's a poor country. If you say UK, USA, the majority of Europe bar the well-known poorer countries taxi drivers, tour operators etc will match the price to what they think you pay at home.

## Set-up a New Uber/ other car hailing app account for discounts

By googling you can find offers with $50 free for new users in most cities for Uber/ Lyft/ Bolt and alike. Just set up a new gmail.com email account to take advantage.

## Where and How to Make Friends

"People don't take trips, trips take people." – John Steinbeck

## Become popular at the airport

Want to become popular at the airport? Pack a power bar with multiple outlets and just see how many friends you can make. It's amazing how many people forget their chargers, or who packed them in the luggage that they checked in.

## Stay in Hostels

First of all, Hostels don't have to be shared dorms, and they cater to a much wider demographic than is assumed. Hostels are a better environment for meeting people than hotels, and more importantly, they tended to open up excursion opportunities that further opened up that opportunity.

## Or take up a hobby

If hostels are a definite no-no for you; find an interest. Take up a hobby where you will meet people. I've dived for years and the nature of diving is you're always paired up with a dive buddy. I met a lot of interesting people that way.

# Small tweaks on the road add up to big differences in your bank balance

### Take advantage of other hotel's amenities

If you fancy a swim but you're nowhere near the ocean, try the nearest hotel with a pool. As long as you buy a drink, the hotel staff will likely grant you access.

### Fill up your mini bar for free.

Fill up your mini bar for free by storing things from the breakfast bar or grocery shop in your mini bar to give you a greater selection of drinks and food without the hefty price tag.

### Save yourself some ironing

Use the steam from the shower to get rid of wrinkles in clothing. If something is creased, leave it trapped with the steam in the bathroom overnight for even better results.

### See somewhere else for free

Opt for long stopovers, allowing you to experience another city without spending much money.

**Wear your heaviest clothes**

on the plane to save weight in your pack, allowing you to bring more with you. Big coats can then be used as pillows to make your flight more comfortable.

**Don't get lost while you're away.**

Find where you want to go using Google Maps, then type 'OK Maps' into the search bar to store this information for offline viewing.

**Use car renting services**

Share Now or Car2Go allow you to hire a car for 2 hours for $25 in a lot of Europe.

**Share Rides**

Use sites like blablacar.com to find others who are driving in your direction. It can be 80% cheaper than normal transport. Just check the drivers reviews.

**Use free gym passes**

Get a free gym day pass by googling the name of a local gym and free day pass.

**When asked by people providing you a service where you are from..**

If there's no price list for the service you are asking for, when asked where you are from, Say you are from a lesser-known poorer country. I normally say Macedonia, and if they don't know where it is, add it's a poor country.  If you say UK, USA, the majority of Europe bar the well-known poorer countries taxi drivers, tour operators etc will match the price to what they think you pay at home.

**Set-up a New Uber/ other car hailing app account for discounts**

By googling you can find offers with $50 free for new users in most cities for Uber/ Lyft/ Bolt and alike. Just set up a new gmail.com email account to take advantage.

# Where and How to Make Friends

"People don't take trips, trips take people." – John Stein-beck

### Become popular at the airport

Want to become popular at the airport? Pack a power bar with multiple outlets and just see how many friends you can make. It's amazing how many people forget their chargers, or who packed them in the luggage that they checked in.

### Stay in Hostels

First of all, Hostels don't have to be shared dorms, and they cater to a much wider demographic than is assumed. Hostels are a better environment for meeting people than hotels, and more importantly they tended to open up excursion opportunities that further opened up that opportunity.

### Or take up a hobby

If hostels are a definite no-no for you; find an interest. Take up a hobby where you will meet people. I've dived for years and the nature of diving is you're always paired up with a dive buddy. I met a lot of interesting people that way.

# When unpleasantries

# come your way...

We all have our good and bad days travelling, and on a bad day you can feel like just taking a flight home. Here are some ways to overcome common travel problems:

### Anxiety when flying

It has been over 40 years since a plane has been brought down by turbulence. Repeat that number to yourself: 40 years! Planes are built to withstand lighting strikes, extreme storms and ultimately can adjust course to get out of their way. Landing and take-off are when the most accidents happen, but you have statistically three times the chance of winning a huge jackpot lottery, then you do of dying in a plane crash.

If you feel afraid on the flight, focus on your breathing saying the word 'smooth' over and over until the flight is smooth. Always check the airline safety record on airlinerating.com I was surprised to learn Ryanair and Easyjet as much less safe than Wizz Air according to those ratings because they sell similarly priced flights. If there is extreme turbulence, I feel much better knowing I'm in a 7 star safety plane.

### Wanting to sleep instead of seeing new places

This is a common problem. Just relax, there's little point doing fun things when you feel tired. Factor in jet-lag to your travel plans. When you're rested and alert you'll enjoy your new temporary home much more. Many people hate the first week of a long-trip because of jet-lag and often blame this on their first destination, but its rarely true. Ask travellers who 'hate' a particular place and you will see that very often they either had jet-lag or an unpleasant journey there.

## Going over budget

Come back from a trip to a monster credit card bill? Hopefully, this guide has prevented you from returning to an unwanted bill. Of course, there are costs that can creep up and this is a reminder about how to prevent them making their way on to your credit card bill:

- To and from the airport. Solution: leave adequate time and take the cheapest method - book before.

- Baggage. Solution: take hand luggage and post things you might need to yourself.

- Eating out. Solution: go to cheap eats places and suggest those to friends.

- Parking. Solution: use apps to find free parking

- Tipping. Solution Leave a modest tip and tell the server you will write them a nice review.

- Souvenirs. Solution: fridge magnets only.

- Giving to the poor. (This one still gets me, but if you're giving away $10 a day - it adds up) Solution: volunteer your time instead and recognise that in tourist destinations many beggars are run by organised crime gangs.

## Price v Comfort

I love traveling. I don't love struggling. I like decent accommodation, being able to eat properly and see places and enjoy. I am never in the mood for low-cost airlines or crappy transfers, so here's what I do to save money.

- Avoid organised tours unless you are going to a place where safety is a real issue. They are expensive and constrain your wanderlust to typical things. I only recommend them in Algeria, Iran and Papua New Guinea - where language and gender views pose serious problems all cured by a reputable tour organiser.

- Eat what the locals do.

- Cook in your Airbnb/ hostel where restaurants are expensive.

- Shop at local markets.

- Spend time choosing your flight, and check the operator on arilineratings.com

- Mix up hostels and Airbnbs. Hostels for meeting people, Airbnb for relaxing and feeling 'at home'.

**Not knowing where free toilets are**

Use Toilet Finder - https://play.google.com/store/apps/details?id=com.bto.toilet&hl=en

**Your Airbnb is awful**

Airbnb customer service is notoriously bad. Help yourself out. Try to sort things out with the host, but if you can't, take photos of everything e.g bed, bathroom, mess, doors, contact them within 24 hours. Tell them you had to leave and pay for new accommodation. Ask politely for a full refund including booking fees. With photographic evidence and your new accommodation receipt, they can't refuse.

**The airline loses your bag**

Go to the Luggage desk before leaving the airport and report the bag missing. Hopefully you've headed the advice to put an AirTag in your checked bag and you can show them where to find your bag. Most airlines will give you an overnight bag, ask where you're staying and return the bag to you within three days. It's extremely rare for Airlines to lose your bag due to technological innovation, but if that happens you should submit an insurance claim after the three days is up, including receipts for everything you had to buy in the interim.

## Your travel companion lets you down

Whether it's a breakup or a friend cancelling, it sucks and can ramp up costs. The easiest solution to finding a new travel companion is to go to a well-reviewed hostel and find someone you want to travel with. You should spend at least three days getting to know this person before you suggest travelling together. Finding someone in person is always better than finding someone online, because you can get a better idea of whether you will have a smooth journey together. Travel can make or break friendships.

## Culture shock

I had one of the strongest culture shocks while spending 6 months in Japan. It was overwhelming how much I had to prepare when I went outside of the door (googling words and sentences what to use, where to go, which station and train line to use, what is this food called in Japanese and how does its look etc.). I was so tired constantly but in the end I just let go and went with my extremely bad Japanese. If you feel culture shocked its because your brain is referencing your surroundings to what you know. Stop comparing, have Google translate downloaded and relax.

## Your Car rental insurance is crazy expensive

I always use carrentals.com and book with a credit card. Most credit cards will give you free insurance for the car, so you don't need to pay the extra. Some unsavoury companies will bump the price up when you arrive. Ask to speak to a manager. If this doesn't resolve, it google "consumer ombudsman for NAME OF COUNTRY." and seek an immediate full refund on the balance difference you paid. It is illegal in most countries to alter the price of a rental car when the person arrives to pickup a pre-arranged car.

## A note on Car Rental Insurance

Always always always rent a car with a credit card that has rental vehicle coverage built into the card and is automatically applied when you rent a car. Then there's no need to buy additional rental insurance (check with your card on the coverage they protect some exclude collision coverage). Do yourself a favour when you step up to the desk to rent the car tell the agent you're already covered and won't be buying anything today. They work on commission and you'll save time and your patience avoiding the upselling.

## You're sick

First off ALWAYS, purchase travel insurance. Including emergency transport up to $500k even to back home, which is usually less than $10 additional. I use https://www.comparethemarket.com/travel-insurance/ to find the best days. If I am sick I normally check into a hotel with room service and ride it out.

## Make a Medication Travel Kit

Take travel sized medications with you:

- Antidiarrheal medication (for example, bismuth subsalicylate, loperamide)

- Medicine for pain or fever (such as acetaminophen, aspirin, or ibuprofen)

- Throat Lozenges

## Save yourself from most travel related hassles

- Do not make jokes with immigration and customs staff. A misunderstanding can lead to HUGE fines.

- Book the most direct flight you can find nonstop if possible.

- Carry a US$50 bill for emergency cash. I have entered a country and all ATM and credit card systems were down. US$ can be exchanged nearly anywhere in the world and is useful in extreme situations, but where possible don't exchange, as you will lose money.

- Check, and recheck, required visas and such BEFORE the day of your trip. Some countries, for instance, require a ticket out of the country in order to enter. Others, like the US and Australia, require electronic authorisation in advance.

- Airport security is asinine and inconsistent around the world. Keep this in mind when connecting flights. Always leave at least 2 hours for international connections or international to domestic. In Stansted for example, they force you to buy one of their plastic bags, and remove your liquids from your own plastic bag.... just to make money from you. And this adds to the time it will take to get through security, so lines are long.

- Wiki travel is perfect to use for a lay of the land.

- Expensive luggage rarely lasts longer than cheap luggage, in my experience. Fancy leather bags are toast with air travel.

## Food

- When it comes to food, eat in local restaurants, not tourist-geared joints. Any place with the menu in three or more languages is going to be overpriced.

- Take a spork - a knife, spoon and fork all in one.

### Water Bottle

Take a water bottle with a filter. We love these ones from Water to Go.

Empty it before airport security and separate the bottle and filter as some airport people will try and claim it has liquids…

### Bug Sprays

If you're heading somewhere tropical spray your clothes with Permethrin before you travel.  It lasts 40 washes and saves space in your bag. A 'Bite Away' zapper can be used after the bite to totally erase it. It cuts down on the itching and erases the bite from your skin.

### Order free mini's

Don't buy those expensive travel sized toiletries, order travel sized freebies online. This gives you the opportunity to try brands you've never used before, and who knows, you might even find your new favourite soap.

## Take a waterproof bag

If you're travelling alone you can swim without worrying about your phone, wallet and passport laying on the beach.

You can also use it as a source of entertainment on those ultra budget flights.

### Make a private entertainment centre anywhere

Always take an eye-mask, earplugs, a scarf and a kindle reader - so you can sleep and entertain yourself anywhere!

### The best Travel Gadgets

### The door alarm

If you're nervous and staying in private rooms or airbnbs take a door alarm. For those times when you just don't feel safe, it can help you fall asleep. You can get tiny ones for less than $10 from Amazon: https://www.amazon.com/Travel-door-alarm/s?k=Travel+door+alarm

### Smart Blanket

Amazon sells a 6 in 1 heating blanket that is very useful for cold plane or bus trips. Its great if you have poor circulation as it becomes a detachable Foot Warmer: Amazon http://amzn.to/2hTYlOP I paid $49.00.

### The coat that becomes a tent

https://www.adiff.com/products/tent-jacket. This is great if you're going to be doing a lot of camping.

### Clever Tank Top with Secret Pockets

Keep your valuables safe in this top. Perfect for all climates.

on Amazon for $39.90

### Optical Camera Lens for Smartphones and Tablets

Leave your bulky camera at home. Turn your device into a high-performance camera. Buy on Amazon for $9.95

**Travel-sized Wireless Router with USB Media Storage**

Convert any wired network to a wireless network. Buy on Amazon for $17.99

**Buy a Scrubba Bag to wash your clothes on the go**

Or a cheaper imitable. You can wash your clothes on the go.

# Hacks for Families

### Rent an Airbnb apartment so you can cook

Apartments are much better for families, as you have all the amenities you'd have at home. They are normally cheaper per person too. We are the first travel guide publisher to include Airbnb's in our recommendations if you think any of these need updating you can email me at philgtang@gmail.com

### Shop at local markets

Eat seasonal products and local products. Get closer to the local market and observe the prices and the offer. What you can find more easily, will be the cheapest.

### Take Free Tours

Download free podcast tours of the destination you are visiting. The podcast will tell you where to start, where to go, and what to look for. Often you can find multiple podcast tours of the same place. Listen to all of them if you like, each one will tell you a little something new.

### Pack Extra Ear Phones

If you go on a museum tour, they often have audio guides. Instead of having to rent one for each person, take some extra earphones. Most audio tour devices have a place to plug in a second set.

### Buy Souvenirs Ahead of Time

If you are buying souvenirs somewhere touristy, you are paying a premium price. By ordering the same exact products online, you can save a lot of money.

## Use Cheap Transportation

Do as the locals do, including weekly passes.

## Carry Reusable Water Bottles

Spending money on water and other beverages can quickly add up. Instead of paying for drinks, take some refillable water bottles.

## Combine Attractions

Many major cities offer ticket bundles where one price gets you into 5 or 6 popular attractions. You will need to plan ahead of time to decide what things you plan to do on vacation and see if they are selling these activities together.

## Pack Snacks

Granola bars, apples, baby carrots, bananas, cheese crackers, juice boxes, pretzels, fruit snacks, apple sauce, grapes, and veggie chips.

## Stick to Carry-On Bags

Do not pay to check a large bag. Even a small child can pull a carry-on.

## Visit free art galleries and museums

Just google the name + free days.

## Eat Street Food

There's a lot of unnecessary fear around this. You can watch the food prepared. Go for the stands that have a steady queue.

## Travel Gadgets for Families

## Dropcam

Are what-if scenarios playing out in your head? Then you need Dropcam.

'Dropcam HD Internet Wi-Fi Video Monitoring Cameras help you watch what you love from anywhere. In less than a minute, you'll have it setup and securely streaming video to you over your home Wi-Fi. Watch what you love while away with Dropcam HD.'

Approximate Price: $139

## Kelty-Child-Carrier

Voted as one of the best hiking essentials if you're traveling with kids and can carry a child up to 18kg.

## Jetkids Bedbox

No more giving up your own personal space on the plane with this suitcase that becomes a bed.

# Safety

"If you think adventure is dangerous, try routine. It's lethal." – Paulo Coelho

Backpacker murdered is a media headline that leads people to think traveling is more dangerous than it is. The media sensationalise the rare murders and deaths of backpackers and travellers. The actual chances of you dying abroad are extremely extremely low.

Let's take the USA as an example. In 2018, 724 Americans **died** from unnatural causes, 167 died from car accidents, while the majority of the other deaths resulted from drownings, suicides, and non-vehicular accidents. Contrast this with the 15,000 murders in the US in 2018, and travelling abroad looks much safer than staying at home.

There are many things you can to keep yourself safe. Here are our tips.

1.  Always check fco.co.uk before travelling. NEVER RELY on websites or books. Things are changing constantly and the FCO's (UK's foreign office) advice is always UP TO DATE (hourly) and **extremely conservative**.

2.  Check your mindset. I've travelled alone to over 180 countries and the main thing I learnt is if you walk around scared, or anticipating you're going to be pickpocketed, your constant fear will attract bad energy. Murders or attacks on travellers are the mainstay of media, not reality, especially in countries familiar with travellers. The only place I had cause to genuinely fear for my life was Papua New Guinea -

where nothing actually happened to me only my own panic over culture shock.

There are many things you can do to stop yourself being victim to the two main problems when travelling: theft or being scammed.

I will address theft first. Here are my top tips:

- Stay alert while you're out and always have an exit strategy.

- Keep your money in a few different places on your person and your passport somewhere it can't be grabbed.

- Take a photo of your passport on your phone in case. If you do lose it, google for your embassy, you can usually get a temporary pretty fast.

- Google safety tips for travelling in your country to help yourself out and memorise the emergency number.

- At hostels, keep your large bag in the room far under the bed/out of the way with a lock on the zipper.

- On buses/trains, I would even lock my bag to the luggage rack.

- Get a personal keychain alarm. The sound will scare anyone away.

- Don't wear any jewellery. A man attempted to rob a friend of her engagement ring in Bogota, Colombia, and in hindsight I wished I'd told her to leave it at home/wear it on a hidden necklace, as the chaos it created was avoidable.

- Don't turn your back to traffic while you use your phone.

- When travelling in the tuktuk sit in the middle and keep your bag secure. Wear sunglasses as dust can easily get in your eyes.

- Don't let anyone give you flowers, bracelets, or any type of trinket, even if they insist it's for free and compliment you like crazy.

- Don't let strangers know that you are alone - unless they are travel friends ;-)

- Lastly, and most importantly -Trust your gut! If it doesn't feel right, it isn't.

# Hilarious Travel Stories

I have compiled these short stories from fellow travellers to pick you up when you're feeling down. Life on the road isn't always easy and we've all had those days when we want to stay in bed and forget the world exists. Laughter is the best way I know to shake those feelings. All people who have shared these stories wanted to remain anonymous. After reading them, I think you'll understand why...

I mentioned my wife earlier, so it's only fair she is the first story. Don't worry, she has given me permission to share.

**A marriage up the wall**

On my third day on a trip to India, I was vomiting so much that I couldn't keep even water down, so I went to a health clinic for tourists. Whilst I was there, I was asked to poop into a jar. The doctor attending me was mid-to-late 40's and very creepy. I decided I'd leave the clinic after my 4th bag of fluids because I felt better and was weirded out by the intense stares of my doctor. As I was paying the bill, the doctor came over, dropped to one knee and asked me to marry him at the desk. I stuttered in shock that I was already married. He was holding a jar of my poo in his hand, stood and then chucked it at the wall. The jar broke open and my watery specimen was literally smeared across the wall as he trudged off. The woman serving me bobbed her head from side to side as if we were discussing the weather and said 'it's not personal madam, you look like his last wife.'

## Glass shame

'I was in Nashville airport in the smoking room. I heard my name being called for my flight, so I rushed out, but instead of rushing through the door, I walked smack into the glass. When I opened the door, the entire departure lounge was roaring with laughter.'

## The Dashing Date

'I had a date with a fellow Brit in Medellin. I went to the bathroom and when I came back, I asked him if he had paid the bill and he replied 'yes'. We were going down some stairs when he suddenly shouted at me to run. Yes, the restaurant staff were running after us because he hadn't paid.'

## A fear of farting in hostels

'When I arrived to stay in my first ever hostel in Adelaide, I realised I had an intense fear of farting in my sleep. I literally gave myself such bad constipation I had to go to hospital. It turns out an enema is worse than hostel farting.'

## What a boob

I fell on the Tube in London getting into a carriage. Unfortunately, I managed to grab a woman's boob on the way to the floor. I was so mortified I walked everywhere else during the trip.'

## Cementing a few laughs

'I was walking on the streets in Singapore when they were fixing the roads. I somehow stepped in fresh cement. I only noticed when my feet became so heavy I thought I had twisted my ankle. The cement got so hard, I had to take them off as I couldn't pick up my feet. Locals were clearly entertained as I walked in my sponge bob square pants socks.

**If you've got a hilarious travel story you'd love to share, email me at** philgtang@gmail.com **All identifying details will be removed.**

# How I got hooked on budget travelling

'We're on holiday' is what my dad used to say to justify getting us in so much debt we lost our home and all our things when I was 11. We moved from the suburban bliss of Hemel Hempstead to a run down council estate in inner-city London, near my dad's new job as a refuge collector, a fancy word for dustbin man. I lost all my school friends while watching my dad go through a nervous breakdown.

My dad loved walking up a hotel lobby desk without a care in the world. So much so, that he booked overpriced holidays on credit cards. A lot of holidays. As it turned out, we couldn't afford any of them. In the end, my dad had no choice but to declare bankruptcy. When my mum realised, he'd racked up so much debt our family unit dissolved. A neat and perhaps as painless a summary of events that lead me to my life's passion: budget travel that doesn't compromise on fun, safety or comfort.

I started travelling full-time at the age of 18. I wrote the first Super Cheap Insider guide for friends visiting Norway - which I did for a month on less than $250. When sales reached 10,000 I decided to form the Super Cheap Insider Guides company. As I know from first-hand experience debt can be a noose around our necks, and saying 'oh come on, we're on vacation' isn't a get out of jail free card. In fact, its the reverse of what travel is supposed to bring you - freedom.

Before I embarked upon writing Super Cheap Insider guides, many, many people told me that my dream was impossible. Travelling on a budget could never be comfortable. I hope this guide has proved to you what I have known for a long-time: budget travel can feel luxurious when you know and use the insider hacks.

And apologies if I depressed you with my tale of woe. My dad is now happily remarried and works as a chef in London at a fancy hotel - the kind he used to take us to!

# A final word...

There's a simple system you can use to think about budget travel. In life, we can choose two of the following: cheap, fast, or quality. So if you want it Cheap and fast you will get a lower quality service. Fast-food is the perfect example. The system holds true for purchasing anything while travelling. I always choose cheap and quality, except at times where I am really limited on time. Normally, you can make small tweaks to make this work for you. Ultimately, you must make choices about what's most important to you and heed your heart's desires.

'Your heart is the most powerful muscle in your body. Do what it says.' Jen Sincero

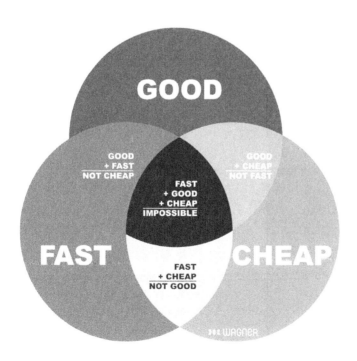

# Our Writers

**Phil Tang** was born in London to Irish immigrant, Phil graduated from The London School of Economics with a degree in Law. Now he travels full-time in search of travel bargains with his wife, dog and a baby and a toddler.

**Ali Blythe** has been writing about amazing places for 17 years. He loves travel and especially tiny budgets equalling big adventures nearly as much as his family. He recently trekked the Satopanth Glacier trekking through those ways from where no one else would trek. Ali is an adventurer by nature and bargainist by religion.

**Michele Whitter** writes about languages and travel. What separates her from other travel writers is her will to explain complex topics in a no-nonsense, straightforward way. She doesn't promise the world. But always delivers step-by-step methods you can immediately implement to travel on a budget.

**Lizzy McBraith**, Lizzy's input on Super Cheap Insider Guides show you how to stretch your money further so you can travel cheaper, smarter, and with more wanderlust. She loves going over land on horses and helps us refine each guide to keep them effective. **If you've found this book useful, please consider leaving a short review on Amazon. it would mean a lot.Copyright**

If you've found this book useful, please select five stars on Amazon, it would mean genuinely make my day to see I've helped you.

# Copyright

Printed in Great Britain
by Amazon

33136938R00106